A Man Was a Real Man in Them Days

A Man Was a Real Man in Them Days

Pioneers of the Llano Estacado--1860 to 1900

By Ruth White Burns and Rose Powers White

A Man Was A Real Man In Them Days
Pioneers of the Llano Estacado--1860 to1900

CreateSpace

Non-fiction/Reference/Publshing

First Edition (July 2012)
First Printing (July 2012)

ISBN: 978-0-9853440-0-9

"A man was a real man in them days, or he didn't last long; and all the women was ladies."

Buster DeGraftenreid, Melrose pioneer

This book is dedicated to the men and women who dared
to make a home in a new and daunting land---and had
the gumption to stay.

Introduction: Rose White---1968

In 1923, when I married R. E. "Eddie" White and came to Portales, New Mexico to live, nobody knew very much about the early history of Roosevelt County. Before the little town of Portales began in 1898, there were no newspapers nearer than Roswell, then the county seat; and people there were not interested in what happened in the far-away northeast corner of the county, which had more contact with Texas than it did with New Mexico. Nobody here knew where Portales got its name. Nobody knew that Portales Springs had been the most famous water hole on the Llano Estacado, nor did they know that Billy the Kid had had a hideout there. Nor did they take any interest in finding out.

For the first two years of our married lives, Eddie and I lived with his mother and stepfather on their tiny ranch three miles northwest of Portales. I soon found that I had married into a veritable history book. Mr. Bob Wood had come to the county with the first big herd of cattle in 1882, and had lived in the area ever since. Mrs. Wood and her two boys, Eddie and Bill, six and four at the time, had come before the town of Portales was begun, and had known all the famous old-time cowboys and ranchers as neighbors and friends. Bob Wood was a great talker, and loved to tell interesting stories about the days when all of our part of the Staked Plains was open prairie, with no fences nor law officers to hamper the freedom-loving pioneers who were the first permanent settlers. His friends were old cowboys, and they loved to discuss the early days too.

It seemed a shame to let all this valuable material go to waste. So, after a short time, I began writing down all the facts of a life that was so different from anything I had known in Las Vegas, New Mexico, where I had grown up. Besides Mr. and Mrs. Wood and Eddie, help came from Joe Beasley, Joe Boren, Sid and Lizzie Boykin, Cooley Urton, Dan McFatter, and Col. Jack Potter of Clayton, N.M.

I don't want to forget Buster DeGraftenreid, who gave me such valuable information about the beginning of the Fort

Sumner Trail. Homesteaders Ella Turner, Grace Henderson, and Mattie Lang were also very helpful

All of these people are dead now, except Eddie, and so the stories could not be replaced, except as they come "second hand" from children and grandchildren of the pioneers. For that reason, this collection, faulty as it is, is the best picture one can find of the early ranch history and of the northern part of Roosevelt County and of the character of the people who settled it.

Rose and Eddie White picnic at Santa Rosa, New Mexico. 1922.
Burns Collection

Introduction: Ruth White Burns---2012

Over the years I have worked intermittently at transcribing the interviews, letters, speeches, and articles that my mother collected during her lifetime and organizing them into a book. I have been distracted at times by family, my return to college, my teaching career, illness, laziness and so forth. Now at age eighty-three, I realize that it is time to "get 'er done." So here goes---

Contents

Chapter 1
The Llano Estacado

To understand the character of the pioneers of Eastern New Mexico, one must realize that the *Llano Estacado*, or Staked Plains, before 1880 was just one vast grassy plain, broken by occasional rolling hills and sandhills. The Llano, often called the "Yarner" by the cowboys, was said to have grass that was high enough to wet a man's boot tops as he rode across the prairie. From the Caprock near Amarillo, Texas, to Ft. Sumner, there was not a single tree, only scrubby bushes and mesquite.

Author and historian, Col. Jack Potter described the Llano Estacado this way: "I have been asked many times for a description of the Llano or Staked Plains and how much country they covered.

"They are an elevated plateau country with the Pecos river paralleling them on the west side for three hundred miles, commencing forty miles north of Fort Sumner at the Mingus Rincon Mesa and the Cu-ne-Va. [sic], a noted spring, which is called the head of the plains.

"The plains are elevated about seven hundred feet above the prairie below.

"The south end of the plains ends east of Pecos, Texas.

"It is a peculiar thing on the east side of the Pecos, for the full length of the plains there is not a creek or river that affords running water at its mouth. On the west side many live streams empty into the Pecos."[1]

According to a soldier with Col. Ranald McKenzie on a foray onto the plains, the llano "appeared to be a vast, almost illimitable expanse of prairie. As far as the eye could reach, not a

---

[1] Jack Potter. "The Staked Plains." *Clovis News-Journal*. June 6, 1936

bush or tree, a twig or stone, not an object of any kind or a living thing, was in sight. It stretched out before us--one uninterrupted plain, only to be compared to the ocean in its vastness."[2]

Water holes were scarce and the danger of being lost on these vast plains was real. It is well-illustrated by the plight of the hunters and Buffalo Soldiers whose tragic march ended at Buffalo Soldier Hill near Causey, New Mexico after several of their company died of thirst. According to John Cook in the book, *The Border and The Buffalo*,[3] even some of the experienced buffalo hunters became lost on the Llano and had to drink the blood of their horses to avoid dying of thirst. Consequently, the eastern plains were the last area of New Mexico to be settled.

Twelve thousand years ago, the plains had been home to the prehistoric Clovis people who hunted the mammoth, dire wolf, and camel. After their disappearance, the only visitors to the Llano up until the 1800s had been the occasional forays of Indians on hunting trips and the visits of the hunters of the buffalo and mustang from the Mexican settlements along the Pecos river.

The first of the Texas cattlemen to come to the eastern New Mexico plains was John Chisum. In 1867 he followed the trail blazed the previous year by Charles Goodnight and brought his nine hundred head of cattle to the Pecos country to establish the Bosque Grande Ranch forty miles south of Ft. Sumner. He maintained a huge cattle operation there with up to a hundred thousand cattle until 1875 when he moved to South Spring River south of Roswell.

Lucien Maxwell and his son Pete had controlled a 36,000 acre ranch at Ft. Sumner with headquarters in the old military buildings until 1884 when the holdings were purchased from the family by four ranchers: Lonny Horn, Sam Doss, D. L. Taylor, and John Lord of the New England Livestock Company.

Doss took over the largest of the three buildings, Taylor the one in the center, and Lord the third. Doss and Taylor took

---

[2] Neeley, Bill. *Quanah Parker and His People.* (Slaton. Brazos Press. 1986.) p. 13.

[3] Cook, John R. *The Border and the Buffalo.* (Topeka: Crane & Co. 1907.) p. 16.

the sheep and most of the horses. Lord, with the New England Livestock Company, took all the cattle with the Maxwell "Heart" brand and hired Jack Potter as foreman. Horn took some of the horses, and located his ranch, called the Pigpen because of the distinctive "#" brand, at the Tules south of the future town of Melrose. The ranchers did not run their animals together, but separated their ranges.[4]

In 1882 Major George W. Littlefield moved a herd from Texas to Chisum's old headquarters at Bosque Grande and established the LFD Ranch under the direction of nephew Phelps White. Maj. Littlefield had numerous cattle operations in Texas under the LIT brand. His practice was to organize a ranch and then place a trusted ranch hand or relative in charge. He formed the Littlefield Cattle Company with Phelps and Tom White, and Charles McCarty, and encouraged them and other associates to form their own ranches.

In 1886 a prolonged drought convinced Littlefield to move his LFD headquarters away from the Pecos to the Four Lakes area on the plains.

In 1881 the Hernandez Brothers had set up a small shack as headquarters for a horse ranch near a natural hidden spring and chinaberry thicket just north of present day Kenna. In 1883 the water rights were sold to Charles S. McCarty, a former trail boss for Littlefield. He built an adobe house and named the ranch T-71.

W. P. "Bill" Littlefield, brother to George W. Littlefield, and others also established ranches in the Kenna area. Descendants of Bill Littlefield and Patrick Henry Boone II still operate his ranch. [5]

A group of Missourians, W. G. Urton, J. D. Cooley, Lee Easley and others formed the Cass Land and Cattle Company in 1884 and set up headquarters at Cedar Canyon northeast of Roswell on the east side of the Pecos. About the same time, J.J. Cox established the Bar-V Ranch on the west side of the river.[6]

---

[4] Jack Potter. letters to Rose White. 1940-1950.

[5] Jayne Taylor. *Kenna, a Ranching Community.* (Elida: 1991.) p. 2.

[6] Cooley Urton. letter to Rose White. 1940.

Doak Good had set up a small cattle operation in Eastern New Mexico in 1880, and he was soon neighbored by Jim Newman of the DZ Ranch, who moved his cattle operation from Yellow House in Texas.

In 1882 the Capitol Freehold Land and Investment Company began to fence huge portions of the Texas Panhandle for the new XIT Ranch. They had received 3,000,000 acres of land in exchange for building the capitol building in Austin. Ranchers who did not have legal title to the land they had been grazing were forced to find other pastures. Consequently, many of them moved across the state line into New Mexico.

Fort Sumner in 1882

Ends facing the parade ground on East.
Erected in 1864 abandoned in 1869, and bought by L B Maxwell
In 1870, and held as a squatter untill 1883, and sold
to Four cattle companies, and shingle roof buildings
were used as ranch head quarters.
The large building on the south has the most historical
value, It was first occupied by the commender of the Fort.
It was in this building where Goodnight and Loving
sontscted the commeander and sold him their herds of steers
to relieve the hunger situation among the Navajo's,In 1866.
The next year 1867 Oliver Loving was brought ther wounded.
L B Maxwell died in this building in 1875, The South east
corner Bldg Known as Pete Maxwell room, Wes where Pat Garrett
contacted Pete Maxwell In 1877 and hired to him as a cow
hand, in same room was where Garrett Killed Billy the Kid
July 14 1881, Fort Sumner was also the end of the trail
For the Whaite Bros, C W, Jim and Bob, In 1884.
With a hard of Texas Cattle.

Old Ft. Sumner military buildings taken over by four ranches.
Letter by Col. Jack Potter.

Mark, Bob, G. W., John, and George Causey. Courtesy of ENMU
Golden Library Special Collections.

Chapter 2
George Causey: Buffalo Hunter, Trail Blazer

Vast herds of buffalo, containing up to five thousand animals, ranged the prairie from South Texas to Canada. They were hunted by the Hispanic explorers in the 1700s and were the main source of food for the Indian tribes. The Indians followed the buffalo as they migrated with the seasons and used every part of the animal: meat, hide, bone and sinew.

As the land along the Rio Grande was occupied, the Hispanic settlers from Las Vegas and Ft. Sumner made annual hunting trips to the plains to hunt the buffalo and antelope for their winter meat. After the meat was "jerked," that is sliced and dried, it would keep indefinitely.

As the Civil War came to a conclusion in the East, the market for buffalo hides skyrocketed and hunters came increasingly to the plains of Texas. Many of these hunters were ex-soldiers looking for the excitement of living on the frontier and hoping to make a "stake."

T. L. "George" Causey, for whom Causey, New Mexico was named, was a rancher, freighter, and most famously, a buffalo hunter. It was his heavy wagons and ox teams hauling the hides to market that made the Portales Road more easily followed by travelers on the Llano Estacado and helped open the way for settlers.

In the 1860s George Causey had worked for the U.S. Government in Kansas hauling supplies to the army outposts with a mule team. He soon formed a buffalo hunting outfit and began following the herds as they moved southward into Texas on their annual migration.

After finding a herd, the usual method of hunting was to set up a stand, as the grazing herd moved slowly and were not startled by occasional gunshots. By shooting from the stand, a hunter could kill a whole herd of animals without moving his position.

After a buffalo was killed, a skinner would come in and skin the animal, stretch the hide, and peg it to the ground to dry. After drying, the hides would be stacked and loaded into the wagons for hauling to a buyer.

Some hunters would salt and smoke the hams for sale to the army, but the meat was usually left to the wolves. Occasionally the tongue and hump would be taken, as they were considered delicacies.

According to John R. Cook,[7] at times five to twenty-five groups of hunters would be strung out around a large herd within sound of each other's rifle shots. Every man carried an ammunition box containing a reloading outfit, consisting of bullet molds, primer extractor, swedge, tamper, patch-paper, and lubricator. The spent rifle shells would be collected and reloaded at night after supper by melting bar lead and adding powder and primers.

Each camp had a heavy two-wheeled cart pulled by six to eight mules or oxen. In addition, there were one or two lighter wagons which were pulled by horses, one containing the provisions and camp outfit.

The camp outfit usually consisted of a couple of Dutch ovens, several large frying pans, two coffee pots, camp kettles, bread pans, a coffee grinder, and tin plates, cups, cutlery, and the all-important sour dough crock. Another wagon carried bedrolls, tools, grindstone, ammunition, and extra guns. The grub box usually contained coffee beans, flour, salt, navy beans, and bacon. The hunter's diet was mostly the ever-present buffalo meat and was only occasionally supplemented by dried or canned fruit.

In the early 1870s, the Kiowa and Comanche Indian tribes roamed the country and made it hazardous for the buffalo hunters. After the fight at Adobe Walls in 1874, Gen. Ranald McKenzie succeeded in rounding up the last of the tribes and taking them to a reservation at Ft. Sill in Oklahoma.

---

[7]John R Cook. *The Border and The Buffalo.* (Topeka: Crane & Co. 1907.) p. 16.

In 1877 George Causey had bought the water rights at Yellow House near the present site of Littlefield, Texas, and established a permanent buffalo hunting camp there. *Casas Amarillas*, called Yellow House, was named for a hundred foot high, flattop yellow bluff with caves in its sides that resembled a house when seen from a distance. Causey built a sod house which came to be widely known as "Causey's Sod House Camp on the Yellow Houses."

The most valuable possessions of the buffalo hunter were his horse and his rifle. The most widely-used rifle was developed by the Sharps Rifle Manufacturing Company especially for hunting buffalo. J. Wright Mooar describes the gun in his book, *Buffalo Days*: "One hundred and ten grains of powder, in a long brass shell, hurled from the beautifully rifled muzzle of the great gun, a heavy leaden missle that in its impact and tearing quality would bring down the biggest bison, if properly aimed, and reached out to incredible distances for rifles of that period. This weapon was billed as a rifle 'that fires today and hits tomorrow.'"[8]

According to Causey's nephew, V. H. Whitlock, "George Causey did most of the killing with a .45-90-caliber buffalo gun that was so heavy he had to use a rest stick to hold it up."

He also quotes Causey's partner, Jeff Jefferson, as saying, "Causey killed more buffaloes in one winter on the Yellow Houses than Buffalo Bill Cody killed in his entire lifetime. But Causey didn't have Ned Buntline for a publicity agent."[9]

Causey is credited with killing the last herd of buffalo on the High Plains. According to Frank Collison in an article in the Amarillo Globe News, Mar. 2, 1941:

"The years of 1877 and 1882 were the height of the buffalo slaughter, with some 7,800 hides taken. After that, the herds were few and far between and most hunters left the country and went on to other occupations. Causey killed the last small herd on the Llano Estacado the winter of 1882. They were killed north and

[8] J. Wright Mooar. *Buffalo Days*. (Abilene: Statehouse Press. McMurray University. 2005) p. 79 & 113.

[9] V.H. Whitlock.*Cowboy Life on the Llano Estacadp (Norman: University of Oklahoma Press. 1970.) p. 9 & 16.*

west of Midland in the sand hills near Cedar Lake, Gaines County, Texas."[10]

With buffalo hunting becoming a losing proposition, Causey turned to salting and drying the buffalo meat for sale and collecting and shipping the innumerable buffalo bones which were in demand back east for fertilizer. He also was involved in mustanging, the catching and breaking of the numerous wild mustangs that roamed the prairie.

Causey sold his squatter's rights at Yellow House to Jim Newman in 1881. He then established a ranch at Ranger Lake where he dug out some of the first shallow wells on the High Plains. He later sold this place to the LFD's and moved on to a location between the present cities of Hobbs and Lovington where he built a large house, outbuildings, and a small store, and ran cattle under the JHB brand.

He and his brother R. L. "Bob" Causey secured a well-drilling outfit and traveled the country drilling water wells for the ranchers and homesteaders who were pouring onto the plains.

At a mustang roundup in 1902, Causey was thrown by a horse and suffered a severe back injury. He spent the next year trying to find medical help and sold all his holdings to pay his doctor bills. He bought a small ranch near Kenna and ended his life there in 1903.

Buster DeGraftenreid has said of Causey, "George Causey was the first man I worked for in 1882 and he was fine in every way, and he sure knew the plains. He could and did travel from lake to lake at night more than in daytime, as he said there was lots of stars to go by and nothing to mislead you. All the old-timers liked George Causey. He never had an enemy."[11]

---

[10] Frank Collison. Article. *Amarillo Globe News*, Mar. 2, 1941.

[11] DeGraftenreid. letter to Rose White. Jan. 24, 1940.

Chapter 4
The Buffalo Soldiers and the Forlorn Hope

A small insignificant hill near Causey, New Mexico is named for a troop of Black soldiers and buffalo hunters who faced days without water while hunting for a band of hostile Indians. The hill was the farthest point reached by the troop before turning back to search for water. Listed on old maps as "Nigger Hill," the name was up-dated in 2004 to Buffalo Soldier Hill by a group of historians led by Oscar Robinson of Portales, and a historical marker was placed near the hill.

This tragedy, which occurred in the last days of July, 1877, is describd in the book, *The Border and the Buffalo,*[12] by John R. Cook, one of the buffalo hunters, and by Paul Carlson in *The Buffalo Soldier Tragedy of 1877.*[13] They disagree on some details, but are mostly in agreement on the main story.

This story begins when a group of Kwahadi Comanches slipped away from the reservation in Indian Territory, Oklahoma, and began a series of depredations over the Staked Plains country of West Texas.

After losing most of their horses to the Indians, a group of buffalo hunters banded together to go onto the Llano Estadado to stay on the trail of the ravaging Comanches, fight them to the finish, and retrieve their stolen stock.

This band of buffalo hunters is known in Plains history as "The Forlorn Hope." The appropriateness of the name may be seen by a review of their activities. The hunters were led by James

---

[12] Cook, John R. *The Border and the Buffalo.* (Topeka: Crane & Co. 1907.) p. 16.

[13] Carlson, Paul H. *The Buffalo Soldier Tragedy of 1877.* (College Station. Texas A & M Press. 2003). p. 118.

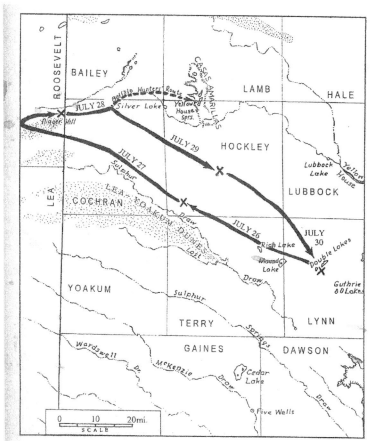

Map 5. Shown here is the route taken by the lost troop expedition from Double Lakes to New Mexico and back again. Courtesy Michael Harter.

Map Courtesy Michael Harter, Texas Tech University
and Paul Carlson.[14]

[14] Carlson. p. 83.

Harvey along with a Mexican guide named Jose' Tafoya. Also among them was John Cook and Bill Benson, later a resident of Portales. This determined group of men tramped back and forth across the plains from early May until the twentieth of July without locating the Indians. On this date they were encamped about twenty-five miles from Big Spring, Texas.

Suddenly the scout encountered a column of soldiers to the southeast of their camp. Upon talking with them they proved to be a colored regiment, Company A, 10th U.S. Cavalry with Capt. Nicholas Nolan commanding. The Indians had given the men the name of "Buffalo Soldiers" due to their dark, curly hair that reminded them of the buffalo's hide.

Nolan related to the now weary, but still determined buffalo hunters, that he had been sent by General Ord to round-up the same band of hostile Indians which they were hunting. Capt. Nolan suggested that his soldiers join with the buffalo hunters and that the hunters simply act as guides while his men would take care of the fighting.

Soon after setting out on the trail, the scouts sent word that five or six Indians bearing a white flag were headed straight for camp. When they arrived, the delegation of Indians was headed by none other than Quanah Parker, son of a Comanche chief and a white mother taken captive by the Indians. At this time he bore a commission from General MacKensie to find his renegade brethren and bring them back to Fort Sill.

Although the buffalo hunters believed that the Indians were camped in the Blue Sandhills, the crafty Quanah indicated that the Indians had gone toward Mustang Springs and that he was going there to seek them. By this ruse he probably succeeded in letting the Indians escape to the north.

On July 26, 1877, while the two commands were in camp at Double Lakes near the present Tahoka, Texas, scouts sent word that the Indians had been sighted and were heading toward Yellow House Canyon. The bugler quickly sounded "Boots and Saddles," and away went the hunters and the soldiers on the trail of the Comanches.

So quickly was the departure taken that many of the group neglected to fill their canteens. The Indians gave their pursuers a strictly dry trail throughout the whole of the insufferably hot day. When darkness came the men dismounted, but made no pretentions for camping, not a drop of water being in the possession of any member of the party.

Their horses were not even unsaddled. At the break of day on July 27, they were again following the dry trail. The Comanches were doing their best to finish their pursuers with thirst. At three o'clock in the afternoon, Captain Nolan called a halt. "Look," he said to the hunters, "I have twenty-five men prostrated. Look at your men, suffering the tortures of the damned. We are all suffering this minute, and if this keeps up much longer, we will each be dethroned of his reason and be a wandering lot of maniacs until death relieves us of our misery."[15]

At this point, the party decided to give up the chase and turn their efforts to finding water. The place at which they turned back is the mound just across the state line in Roosevelt County, New Mexico. It is signifiant to note that exhausted men had been dropping from the ranks all through this second maddeningly hot July day.

Hunters and soldiers all turned and started back northeast toward Silver Lake. When the night of July 27 came, a more wretched group of men could not have been found than these hunters and soldiers who lay down in scattered groups in the vastness of the plain, "suffering the tortures of the damned." There were stragglers all about, for miles back on the trail.

Daylight of July 28 came, but no water. Captain Nolan, almost beside himself, ordered his lieutenant to set his compass for the southeast and head toward Double Lakes. The hunters, more knowledgable of the plains, believed that water could be found nearer at Casas Amarillas, Yellow House Springs. Nolan stated that the hunters were hopelessly lost and that they were going to their destruction in trying to reach Casas Amarillas. Thus the hunters and the soldiers parted company, the hunters going northeast and the soldiers, southeast.

Some of the hunters did succeed in reaching Yellow House Springs that day and heroically took water back to their

---

[15] Cook. p. 268.

struggling companions. Scenes almost indescribable took place along the trail. Horses were killed and the blood drunk by some of the men. Lower jaws of men fell, their tongues swelled and protruded. Finally, however, all of the buffalo hunters were succored and reached water.

The soldiers did finally reach the Double Lakes on July 30, eighty-six hours without water, before which they killed and drank the blood from twenty-two of their horses. According to military records, four of the black soldiers perished.[16] The legend around Roosevelt County always was that a group of them were left on the hill, and that they either died there of thirst or were slaughtered there by the Comanches, but over the years, no evidence of this has been found.

It is certain that the old buffalo hunter Bill Benson, who was a member of the party of hunters taking part in this tragic exploit, always pointed out Negro Hill as the westernmost point reached by the soldiers. When the parties separated, white-haired old Benson had gone with the soldiers, hoping to convince them to follow the hunters. Unable to change their course, he went northeast alone towards Yellow House Canyon and was a full four days without water.

When he finally reached water, he was "crazy as a bug. It was three weeks before his mind was thoroughly restored."[17] He was a long-time resident of Portales, the Benson Addition in north Portales being named for him.[18]

Later testimony revealed that the Indians had indeed been camped in the Blue Sandhills, only seven miles from the place where the troop turned back. They had known of the troop's presence at all times, and were led back to the reservation by Quanah as soon as the soldiers turned back to Texas.[19]

---

[16] Carlson. p. 121.

[17] Cook. p. 283.

[18] White, Rose. *Place Names: Nigger Hill.* (Western Folklore. vol. IX. June 1950.University of California Press.)

[19] Carlson. p. 109.

Thus we see that this small grassy hill on the face of the flat uninteresting-looking prairie, has a name that commemorates one of the most dramatic tragedies of all the troublesome early history of the Staked Plains.

BUFFALO-HUNTERS FIGHTING COMANCHES AND APACHES, MARCH 18, 1877, ON THE STAKED PLAINS.

Buffalo Soldiers and hunters fighting Indians 1877 on the Staked Plains. *The Border and the Buffalo.*

Re-enactment of Buffalo Soldier Troop. ENMU Golden Library
Special Collections.

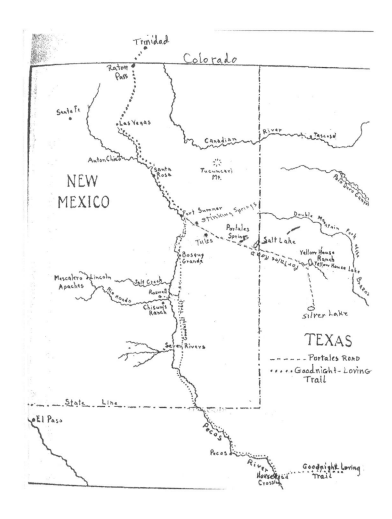

The Portales Road or the Ft. Sumner Trail and the
Goodnight-Loving Trail. Burns Collection.

Chapter 4
Cattle Trails

The first cattle were brought to the New World by the Spanish explorers and had greatly multiplied in the mild climate of Texas. Before the Civil War, cattlemen had shipped their stock east by ship, but during the war, the Texas ports were blockaded by the Union Forces.

As the war went on, most able-bodied Texans left their homes to fight for the Confederacy and their cattle were left to run wild. After the war, it was estimated that between three and four million longhorn cattle were running loose on the plains and in the brushy thickets of Texas. Enterprising Texans realized that they could make a profit by trailing these cattle to northern railheads.

Jack Potter became an authority on cattle trails, having traveled over most of them. For many years after his first introduction to trail-herding at the age of sixteen, he was trail boss for herds traveling north, and became an expert on cattle and cattle trails. He described the various trails in his book, *Cattle Trails of the Old West*.[20]

He said, "The best cows on the range at the close of the War were quoted at from three to five dollars a head with no takers. In fact, the price was so low that thousands of cattle were killed for hide and tallow alone. In 1865 a high grade, matured animal was worth ten times as much in some Northern states as in Texas. It was only natural then that the stockman of the Southwest looked to the north for his market.

"If the cattleman could reach the end of the railroad line, he could ship by rail to northern markets. However, the

---

[20] Jack Potter. *Cattle Trails of the Old West.* (Clayton: Laura R. Krehbiel & Leader Press..1935) p. 9-10.

difficulties in reaching the northern buyer were great. Hundreds of miles of unknown Indian country had to be traversed, with no assurance of arriving at the journey's end."

So in 1866 the first herds of cattle made their way north, and for the next thirty years, until the railroad came to Texas, millions of cattle were trailed out of Texas to the northern railheads.

Perhaps the most famous in song and story, the *Chisholm Trail*, was blazed in 1865 by Jess Chisholm from Wichita, Kansas to the Washita River near what would later be Anadarko, Oklahoma, to fulfill a Government contract to move a group of Indians to the reservation there.

There has been much confusion as to where this trail started, but according to the Trail Driver's Association, it never entered Texas. Herders coming up the *Eastern Trail* intersected the *Chisholm* at the Washita River near Anadarko, Indian Territory, now Oklahoma.

The *Eastern Trail* was blazed in 1867 mostly by Confederate soldiers driving their cattle north to Abilene, Kansas.

In 1866 the *Goodnight-Loving Trail* was blazed by Charles Goodnight and Oliver Loving to herd cattle from Central Texas to Ft. Sumner to feed the Indians confined at Bosque Redondo. They used various routes at different times, sometimes on the east side of the Pecos, sometimes on the west.

In 1876 the *Western Trail* was established as a more direct route to market, bypassing Indian Territory. This trail was one-thousand miles in length, extending from Matamoros on the Gulf Coast of Texas to Dodge City, Kansas and on to Ogalalla and the Red Cloud Agency in Nebraska.

The *Jim Stinson Trail* was blazed in 1882 by Jim Stinson, manager of the New Mexico Land and Cattle Company, who drove cattle from west central Texas to the Estancia Valley in New Mexico. This trail entered New Mexico at Salt Lake and followed the *Portales Road*, passing by Tierra Blanca, the Tules near Melrose, Stinking Springs, Ft. Sumner and on west to Arizona.

In 1883 the *Potter-Bacon Cut-off* was pioneered by Potter when herding cattle north from San Antonio. Following the instructions of his boss, Alfred T. Bacon, Potter left the *Western*

Trail and detoured around Charles Goodnight's ranch at Palo Duro, saving about twenty days' time.

Wrote Potter, "I have seen this trail marked on different maps and called by different names. I am sure I blazed this trail and it should be named the *Potter and Bacon Trail*. Bacon mapped it and Potter drove it."

In 1884, due to an outbreak of Tick Fever among the Texas cattle, the *National Trail* was blazed to detour around Kansas. It left the *Western Trail* at the southwest corner of Kansas and proceeded on north to Ogallala, Nebraska.

The route known as the *Ft. Sumner Trail* or the *Portales Road* went from Singer's Store near the present town of Lubbock to Salt Lake now Grulla Wildlife Refuge to Portales Springs to the Tules near present Melrose to Stinking Springs near Tiaban to Ft. Sumner

J. Frank Dobie, in his book, *The Longhorns*, estimated that up to 10,000,000 cattle and 1,000,000 horses were driven up the trail from Texas from the time the Civil War ended until the coming of the railroads.[21]

---

[21] J. Frank Dobie. *The Longhorns*. (Boston: Little, Brown & Co. 1941.) p. 85.

Jack Potter. Cowboy Historian.
ENMU Golden Library Special Collections.

Chapter 5
Jack Potter: Cowboy Historian

One of the most amazing and colorful characters to emerge on the western scene was Jack Potter, famous cowboy, author, historian and all-around good storyteller. He was affectionately known as "Col." Jack Potter, although he was never in the military. He cut an imposing figure, being over six feet tall and of a stocky build.

Unlike many of the uneducated cowhands of that day, Potter was well-spoken and could read and write in spite of a lack of formal education. His only schooling was three four-month terms in a one-room log cabin, but he often carried his Blue Back Speller in his saddle bag and studied it at night on the trail. Many of the old-timers had left home in their early teens, and, like my own step-grandfather Bob Wood, could neither read nor write, but could count a herd on the trail and never miss a horn.

Rose White had contacted Col. Potter in doing research on the history of the High Plains area. She found him to be an invaluable source of information, as he had traveled the Portales Road many times. He was well-acquainted with all the old-timers of the day and had a fantastic memory. For many years, she carried on a voluminous correspondence with him; and he visited in her home in Portales for several days in 1949, regaling her and her family with his many stories of the Llano.

Jack Potter was born at Prairie Lee, Caldwell County, Texas, December 11, 1864, and moved to Kendall County at the age of five. He was the fifth son of a family of eight boys and six girls. His father was a famous early day preacher who was a circuit rider and minister to the cow camps.

According to Potter, "My father was a militant pioneer parson, Andrew Jackson Potter, who wrote his name large in the annals of Texas frontier evangelism."[22]

The "Fighting Parson," as he was known throughout Texas, had fought in the confederate army and was known to lay a pistol on the pulpit next to his Bible when in doubt about the peaceful intent of his rugged congregation.

In one incident related by southwest author, J. Frank Dobie, the parson noted the absence of any men at his church service. As soon as the service was over, Parson Potter hied himself to the saloon, and in a booming voice declared,

"Why, I was thinking all the women in this town were widows. I see they're not. I believe I'll preach here right now and give the men a chance to listen," which he proceeded to do and took up a fine collection at the end.[23]

Jack Potter grew up watching the stage coaches and freight caravans as they passed by his home on the main road from San Antonio to El Paso. Later, as the thundering herds of long-horned cattle began to wind their way north, his lifelong love of cattle and ranching was born. He writes, "Then and there, I made up my mind that nothing but a cowboy's life was worthy of my talents."

At the age of ten or twelve, he got a job as "brush hand" at one dollar per day, and at the age of sixteen, he was given a job as assistant driver with a big herd. Within two years, he was promoted to trail boss with a herd headed for Cheyenne, Wyoming. More than half a century, he "watched the longhorns browse the hills and valleys and followed them hundreds of miles over trails."

Life was not easy for a young inexperienced cowhand. On one of his first trips with a trail herd, Potter came down with the chills from long hours and poor food, and was dropped off at a way camp with a grouchy old trail-cutter. It was customary to

---

[22] Jack Potter. *Lead Steer and Other Tales.* (Clayton: Leader Press. 1939.) p. 13.

[23] J. Frank Dobie. "Belling the Lead Steer." Jack Potter in *Lead Steer and Other Tales.* (Clayton: Leader Press. 1939. p. 4.

cut out all lame cattle and sick cowhands and leave them to recuperate before hitting the most difficult part of the journey.

The situation looked pretty bad to Potter. He wrote, "In the little dugout of the trail-cutter, which was about 12x12, there was a cowboy lying flat on his back with a broken leg which had been dressed by using a splint. He had it lying in a trough. On a rise a few hundred feet in front of the dugout was a fresh made grave, and several head of lame cattle and horses--with a few dead ones near by."

Potter shook so badly with the chills that the lame cowboy complained and the old trail-cutter got up cursing all doctors.

"He said he had a remedy that would cure the chills in twenty-four hours. He got a can of cayenne pepper and gave me two tablespoons full and told me to repeat the dose at the regular time that the chill should strike me. That was the last chill I had. In two days time, with my pockets full of cayenne pepper, I bade farewell to the trail-cutter and the lame cowboy and hit the trail."

So for the rest of his days, Potter followed his dream of living the cowboy life. He continued to work as a cowhand with herds heading from Texas to the railheads in the north, and was soon promoted to Trail Boss.

He became head Trail Boss for the New England Livestock Company, and in 1886 was made foreman of their breeding ranch at Ft. Sumner. The Fort at Bosque Redondo [Round Grove] was erected in 1864 to oversee the nine thousand Apache and Navajo Indians captured and confined there by the military.

The camp was a disaster from the beginning and was abandoned when the Indians simply left and walked back to their old homes. In 1870 the fort buildings were purchased by Lucien Maxwell and his son Pete and were sold in 1883 to several cattlemen, including Sam Doss, L. B. Horn, D. L. Taylor, and J. L. Lord of the New England Livestock Company.

Of a photograph of the Fort buildings taken in 1883, Potter stated, "The large building on the south has the most historical value. It was first occupied by the Commander of the Fort.

"It was in this building where Charles Goodnight and Oliver Loving contacted the Commander and sold him their herds of steers to relieve the hunger situation among the Navajos in 1866. The next year, 1867, Loving was brought there wounded."[24]

The incident happened when Loving and Goodnight were taking a herd of cattle north. Loving and One-armed Billy Wilson went ahead to scout out the trail. They had been advised by Goodnight to travel only at night, but they got in a hurry and proceeded in the daytime.

They were attacked by Indians and barely escaped with their lives. Wilson managed to walk the eighty miles back to the herd with his bare feet bleeding, and being constantly harassed by wolves. Loving was struck in the arm and side by arrows, but made it to Ft. Sumner with the help of some passing sheepherders. He contracted gangrene in his arm and died there. Goodnight promised Loving that he would be buried in Texas, so he carried the body the long trip back to Weatherford to be laid to rest.[25]

Larry McMurtry used this incident in his book, *Lonesome Dove*,[26] as the inspiration for the account of the death of Gus McCrae and the trip back to Texas with his body by Captain Woodrow Call.

Of the Ft. Sumner buildings, Potter continues, "L. B. Maxwell died in this building in 1875. The southeast corner known as the Pete Maxwell Room was where Pat Garrett contacted Pete Maxwell in 1877 and hired to him as a cow hand. In the same room was where Garrett killed Billy the Kid, July 14, 1881."

After retiring from the cattle business, Potter moved to Clayton, New Mexico, where he served as Justice of the Peace. He

---

[24] Potter. letter to Rose White. 1948.

[25] J. Evetts Haley. *Charles Goodnight.* (Norman: University of Olkahoma Press, 1936.) p. 182.

[26] Larry McMurtry, *Lonesome Dove.* (New York: Simon & Schuster. 1985.)

was elected to the New Mexico State Legislature in 1932 and again in 1934.

Of his election campaign, Potter wrote, "I believe I have told more lies and talked more Spanish and eaten more chili than I ever did in my life before in such a short time.

"I may get hard to hold, but I had rather have the honor of having been a common drag driver on one of the northern cattle trails than be a 'dam' legislator. Poetry has been written about the longhorn and the men that drove him, but who ever heard of poetry about a common legislator?"

Potter had a fabulous memory and never forgot a man or a steer. He wrote numerous articles for newspapers and magazines and published two books, "Lead Steer" and "Cattle Trails of The Old West."

Potter cut an impressive figure in his black suit and large white western hat. Famous southwestern author, J. Frank Dobie, has said of him, "Just to look at him made me realize that I had met a man--and such men are not common--summing up in himself the whole trail driver and range tradition."[27]

Well-known New Mexico poet S. Omar Barker immortalized Potter in several poems, among them, "Jack Potter's Courtin'" and "Jack Potter's Talkin' Steer," in which he described Potter:

> "His job was drivin' long horns and he set up in his kack,
> As sure and straight as if he wore a ramrod in his back.
> He knowed the ways of cattle from their burrtails to their
>   ears
> 'twas even said he had the knack of understanding steers
> The same as if they spoke in words instead of with the
>   eye
> But when it comes to women, he was spooky-like and
>   shy."[28]

---

[27] Dobie. p 5.

[28] S. Omar Barker. "Jack Potter's Courtin' ." (Phoenix: Cowboy Miner Productions. 1998.) p. 70

Potter died November 21, 1951 in Clayton, New Mexico at age 86 and is buried there.

Rose White and Col. Jack Potter. 1949. Burns Collection.

Chapter 6
Los Portales, Portales Springs

One of the most interesting of the historic spots in Eastern New Mexico is *Los Portales*, or Portales Springs, the site of tragedies and adventures as exciting as any of the tales of the wild and woolly West.

In the 1800s the caliche cliffs stood out sharply in the otherwise grassy plain of the Llano Estacado. From the north, one saw only a gently rising hill, but from the south side looking back, one saw that the caliche outcropping stretched for about half a mile in a wavering line of white rock against the gray-green grass and gray earth.

At the foot of the ten to twelve-foot bluff, the land dropped away gradually to a large, marshy lake surrounded by tules, slender reeds similar to cattails. The caliche cliffs jutted out to form porches over several large caves. Springs splashed out from beneath these porches to replenish the lake. A wonderful variety of animals frequented the lake.

The most prominent were the buffalo, which traveled in herds of up to five or six thousand. There were antelope, wild mustangs, lobo wolves, coyotes, cranes, ducks, geese, prairie chickens, plover, curlew, rabbits, skunks, badgers, fox, weasels, and prairie dogs. Wild celery and water cress grew around the edges of the lake.

To understand the importance of Portales Springs, one must understand the scarcity of water on the vast plain. The Llano Estacado, which extended into the Texas Panhandle, had very few sources of water; and the few lakes scattered across the plains were often dry during part of the year. From Yellow House near Littlefield, Texas, there were very few dependable sources of water until one reached the Pecos River. The usual trail led from Yellow House to Salt Lake across the border in New Mexico, to

"Los Portales." Painting by Lawanda Calton. 2012.

Portales Springs, to Tierra Blanca Lake, to the Tules near the future town of Melrose, to Stinking Spring, to the Pecos River at Ft. Sumner. This was a distance of eighty miles from Salt Lake to Ft. Sumner with no other watering places in between.

Wherever there was water, human visitors came. The earliest of these travelers of the Llano Estacado were the Indians: Apache, Navajo, and Comanche, who came to hunt the plentiful buffalo and antelope.

Later Hispanics from the Rio Grande settlements of Las Vegas and Santa Fe made annual trips to the plains to salt and dry meat for the winter. *Mesteñeros* came to catch the wild mustangs that roamed the prairie. It was probably these early hunters who first called the springs "Los Portales," Spanish for "The Porches."

Jack Potter has said, "In the 1880s, there was enough water at the Springs to water ten thousand cattle. Antelope hunters could kill all they wanted by taking advantage of the antelope's curiosity.

"The hunters would make a wooden sled and drag it behind a horse down to the lake. The antelope would come in droves to see what this peculiar thing was, and the hunters could kill them by the hundreds."[29]

As the tribes were pushed out of Texas by settlers after the Civil War, the route was used by marauding Indian bands who escaped into the deserts of New Mexico after raids in Texas.

The militia used the trail that went past the springs, and often detachments from Ft. Union or Ft. Bascom would water at the springs while in pursuit of raiding bands of Indians. The despised *Comancheros*, men who traded guns, ammunition and other supplies to the Indians for stolen horses, rested at the lake on their way back to Las Vegas or Texas.

An article in the Daily New Mexican of March 3, 1871, speaks of this "illicit and reprehensible traffic:"

"The soldiers appear to be doing good work; they have captured a great many cattle, and have prevented the Comanche leaders from passing; they, the Comanche, have fortified themselves at a place known as the Portalles, [sic], have erected works of defense, and otherwise made every preparation to fight."[30]

Portales Springs was one of the most important watering holes on this trail. Although it followed the old military route, it was not used very frequently. Most cattlemen and other travelers preferred to follow the Goodnight-Loving Trail which originally came into New Mexico south of Carlsbad and traveled up the west side of the Pecos River to Ft. Sumner.

The Goodnight-Loving Trail had been blazed in 1866 by Charles Goodnight and Oliver Loving when they herded their Texas cattle to Ft. Sumner to feed the Indians impounded at Bosque Redondo.

---

[29] Potter, Col. Jack. interview by Rose White. September 29, 1949.

[30] Article. *Daily New Mexican*. March 3, 1871.

Consequently, the remoteness of Portales Springs made it a perfect place for illicit activity, and it became a favorite meeting place of the Comancheros with the Indians, and a safe hide-out for those avoiding the law. Billy the Kid often used the Portales Springs as a rendevouz.

DZ cowboy Dan McFatter said, "The caves were commonly known as The Caves of Billy the Kid. In those days the walls were as black as a pot from his fires. The road wasn't traveled very much in them days, only by horse and cattle thieves like Billy and his gang. People going by could not see back into the cave, and you may be sure that no one was going back into it to see if Billy was inside."[31]

Charles Siringo was pursuing the Kid to recover cattle stolen in Texas, when he wrote in his book, *A Texas Cowboy*:

"The second day after leaving Stinking Springs [near Taiban], we came to the 'Kid's' noted 'Castle' at Los Potales [sic], on the western edge of the great Llano Estacado."

He goes on to describe the scene:

"Los Potales [sic] is a large alkali lake, the water of which is unfit for man or beast. [Though alkali, the water could be drunk.] But on the north side of the lake is two nice cool springs which gurgle forth from a bed of rock near the foot of 'Kid's' Castle'--a small cave in the cliff.

"In front of the cave is a stone corral about fifty feet square; and above the cave on the level plain is several hitching posts. Outside of those things mentioned there is nothing but a level prairie just as far as the eye can reach. We found one hundred head of [stolen] cattle, mostly from the Canadian River, but a few from as far north as Denver, Col."[32]

Billy the Kid would take cattle stolen from New Mexico ranchers, such as John Chisum, and water them at Portales Springs while trail-herding them to Tascosa to sell. In his book, *The Authentic Life of Billy the Kid*, Pat Garrett writes of an attempt to capture Billy in 1880:

---

[31] Dan McFatter. Interview by Rose White. 1939.

[32] Charles Siringo. *A Texas Cowboy*. (Chicago: M. Umbdenstock & Co. 1885.)
    p. 156.

"We returned to Fort Sumner, stayed one night, and...started for the Kid's stronghold, Los Portales, where he was wont to harbor his stolen livestock. This place was sixty miles east of Ft. Sumner, and was the veritable castle so graphically described by newspaper correspondents, with its approaches impassible except to the initiated and inaccessible and impregnable to foes.

"Los Portales is but a small cave in a quarry of rock, not more than fifteen feet high, lying out and obstructing the view across a beautiful level prairie. Bubbling up near the rocks are two springs of cool clear water capable of furnishing an ample supply for at least one thousand head of cattle. There is no building or corral; all the signs of habitation are a snubbing post, some rough working utensils, and a pile of blankets--just that and nothing more.

"The Kid was supposed to have had about 60 head of cattle in the vicinity of Los Portales, all but eight of which were stolen from John Newcomb at Agua Azul. On our visit we found only two cows and calves and a yearling, but we heard afterwards that the Kid had moved his stock to another spring about fifteen miles east."[33]

Jack Potter writes in an article in the Union County Leader, Clayton, New Mexico, of Billy the Kid's last visit to Portales Springs before he was killed by Pat Garrett at Ft. Sumner:

"He and his men had a clever system worked out whereby members of his gang could communicate with each other by certain hieroglyphics on the walls of rock surrounding Portales Spring. He stated that he had been there three times, but had been disappointed each time. After visiting a few days at his old rendezvous, Portales Spring, and finding no answer to his code message which he had scrolled on the sandy rock at the spring.

"He must have took a scare or else had an ugly vision in his sleep. Because on the morning of July 14, 1881, he awakened

---

[33] Pat Garrett. *The Authentic Life of Billy The Kid.* (New York: McMillan Co. 1927.) p. 148-149.

and saddled his mount and started hurriedly on his last ride over the famous old Portales Road, eighty miles to Fort Sumner."[34]

As history has recorded, Billy was shot by Pat Garrett as Pat conversed with Pete Maxwell in his darkened bedroom on July 14, 1881, bringing to an end Billy's flamboyant career.

In the 1880s the trail past Portales Springs, commonly known as the Ft. Sumner Trail or the Portales Road, became more widely used. Buster DeGraftenreid, who was a prominent old-time cowboy of the Melrose community, describes it thus:

"Now my father moved to New Mexico in 1882 over this new route across the plains to Ft. Sumner. I was about 14 years old and in November 1883, I worked for George Causey in his buffalo camp north of Yellow House Canyon [near Littlefield, Texas].

"George Causey was the last buffalo hunter on the plains. He had a big freight outfit of oxen; freighted from Las Vegas and Fort Worth. He told me his was the first wagons that crossed the plains. He hunted and killed buffalo at Yellow House and in the spring of 1879 loaded his hides and meat, seven wagons with trailer wagons and seven to eight yokes of steer to a wagon. He said he had made the trip horseback and knew the way from Yellow House to Silver Lake to Salt Lake to Portales Lake to Tierra Blanca to Big Tules; from Tules to Stinking Spring to Taiban to Ft. sumner up the Pecos to Las Vegas.

"You see the big cattle herds couldn't cross the plains only in a rainy season when there was rain water in the lakes.

"In 1879, after George Causey went from the Yellow House to Ft. Sumner with his big bull team, he made such a plain road people began to cross the plains."[35]

So the stage was set for the influx of new settlers and the establishment of the first ranches, the DZ, H-Bar, Pig Pen, LFD, T-71, and others.

---

[34] Jack Potter. "Tragedies of the Portales Road."*Union County Leader.* Clayton, N.M. 1942.

[35] Buster DeGraftenreid, letter to Rose White. Jan. 11, 1940.

Portales Springs about 1880. ENMU Golden LIbrary
Special Collections.

Portales Springs 2000. Photo by Mike Burns Jr.

Doak Good at Portales Springs. Old Postcard. Courtesy ENMU
Golden Library Special Collections.

Chapter 7
Doak Good at Los Portales

It is an interesting fact that a Washington scandal involving a U.S. Senator from Arkansas brought the first permanent resident down the Ft. Sumner Trail to the Portales Valley.

Doak Good, a thirty-three-year-old suspicious-natured bachelor, had a contract to carry the mail between Singer's Store, now Lubbock, Texas, and Ft. Sumner and all points in between. This was part of what came to be known as "The Star Route Swindle," a nationwide scheme organized by Senator S. W. Dorsey and others to get money from the government for false or unnecessary mail routes. Certainly Good only carried the mail when he felt like it, perhaps every two or three months.

About 1880 or 1881, as Good passed by Portales Springs on his mail route, he decided the springs and the adjacent lake would be a good place to run a few cattle. He set up camp in the caves under the overhanging caliche porches and later built a house and sheds out of waste rock on top of the bluff. His new home had a loft in it with a half-window to the east.

Historian Jack Potter has said, "Good was of a slender build. His mustache was light and barely covered his upper lip and it was a blond color. In fact when I first met Doak Good, you could of passed him off for a big blond nester girl."[36]

Good ran three hundred to four hundred cattle at the Springs, branded "GOOD" and later "FX". He led a peaceful life until the XIT Ranch across the Texas line began to fence in their range and push out the smaller cattlemen.

In 1882 Jim Newman began to move his cattle from Yellow House near the present Lubbock, Texas, to the Salt Lake

---

[36] Jack Potter. letters to Rose White. 1941-1950.

near Arch. The lake water was salty, and as more cattle were brought in, there was not enough water for Newman's large herd and his cattle tended to drift over to Portales Springs. Good complained that the nearby ranch did not have enough water and that Newman's cattle were coming over and drinking his water and eating his grass.

Resentment simmered and trouble was bound to follow. Once twenty-five of Good's fat steers were shot and he swore that Jim Newman had done it. Finally, at a roundup one spring, Good openly accused Newman of trying to run him out of the country. They emptied their guns at each other, but neither was hit. Good wanted to keep on fighting and begged for more cartridges. Newman got around the other side of the herd to reload his gun; but Doak's horse took a notion to run away about then; and by the time Good got back, the DZ boys had gotten Jim away.[37]

One of the legendary shooting scrapes that took place was the one between Good and Gabe Henson. All of the details may or may not be true, but this is what was sworn to by the cowboys who were there at the time, including my step-grandfather, Bob Wood.

A man named Gabe Henson moved a small herd of cattle onto the open range to the east of Portales Springs, and Doak was soon quarreling with the newcomer. Good thought Newman had put Henson up to moving in. Henson showed up at Good's place one morning and called for him to "come out and shoot it out." Henson hid out behind the shed and began taking potshots at Good.

Good was convinced that Newman had sent Henson to kill him and commenced shooting out the window with his old Sharp's buffalo gun. The men continued to shoot at each other all morning.

According to DZ cowboy Dan McFatter, "At noon, Doak sent Henson's dinner out to him. Henson ate it; then the shooting began again. Finally Henson got tired of this, and yelled at Good to come on out. This Doak refused to do.

[37] Bob Wood, interview by Rose White, 1932.

"Then Gabe came out and sat down in front of the *choza,* or shed, probably figuring that he would sit there till Doak did come out. Then Doak fired from the window and killed him.

"But the cowboys who picked Gabe up and carried his body home, said that there wasn't a drop of blood anywhere on Henson's body; the bullet wound didn't bleed at all. We all believed that the dinner was really what killed him. Doak had poisoned it and Gabe was dead before he shot him."[38]

Cooley Urton of the Bar-V Ranch said, "I heard Doak Good tell my father about killing the man at Portales Springs. He declared that he hated it so bad because he had shot the sight off Henson's gun. Doak said, 'He didn't have a chance. If I had known he didn't have any sights on his gun, I never would have shot him.' Henson hung around for two days trying to shoot Good. Finally Good sent his breakfast out to him before he shot him.

"The Bar-V outfit leased the springs from Doak Good and had a winter camp in his house in the 90's. Doak was in Roswell at that time and was [there] at times during the late 90's. He had a Roswell paper sent to him in Washington or Oregon for several years after leaving here."[39]

After Newman bought the cattle from Henson's widow, Good was more convinced than ever that Newman had planned the whole thing.

McFatter described Doak thus: "When Jim fired me in the spring of 1886, I went to work for Doak. I worked for him for about three months, hauling mesquite roots for wood. When I worked for Doak, he was about thirty-three years old; had medium brown hair, grey eyes; was about five feet eight inches tall. At times he carried the mail from Ft. Sumner to some fort in Texas; maybe once in two or three months.

"His house was a two-room adobe on the north side of Portales Springs about fifty steps or yards west of the cave of Billy the Kid. He did not have a family."

---

[38] Dan McFatter. interview by Rose White. 1939.

[39] Cooley Urton. letter to Rose White. 1949.

In commenting on Doak's suspicious nature, McFatter said, "In the spring of 1886, Doak had three or four hundred cattle. He was always asking me how many of his cattle Jim Newman had stole. I would answer, 'He left for Sweetwater two or three days after I started working for him. He never stole any that I know of.' But he wasn't satisfied. He'd ask me again and again."

When asked of Doak's reputation, McFatter said, "I know one thing: Doc Winfrey at the H-Bar was always as afraid as death of Doak. Once when Winfrey had to go to claim some cattle east of Doak's house, he went 'way around, four or five miles out of his way, so as to miss Doak's house."

"Billy the Kid at Los Portales." Drawing by Pat Burns.

Chapter 8
The XIT Changes the Llano

One of the biggest land deals in United States history helped bring about the settlement of the barren plains of Eastern New Mexico.

In 1879 brothers Charles and John Farwell and others organized a syndicate of eastern investors and agreed to build the red granite capitol building in Austin in exchange for title to 3,000,000 acres of land in the Texas Panhandle. This grant took in portions of ten counties ranging from Yellow House near Littlefield in the South to the Oklahoma Panhandle in the North. The brand of this new ranch was "XIT," so XIT became the name of the ranch.

In 1882 when they began surveying and fencing this vast area, it forced the settlers who had only squatter's rights to move on. Many of them moved their cattle west into New Mexico.

Two of the pioneers who first migrated to the high plains area were the Carter and the Riley Families.

The Carter Family
The Carters left their holdings at Black Water, or Agua Prieta, between Salt Lake and Spring Lake, Texas in 1881, and settled about ten miles west of the present site of Portales at Tierra Blanca Lake, so named because of the "White Earth" which surrounded it..

The first names of the parents are not known, but a deed filed in 1892 lists the owner as W.W. Carter. According to Jack Potter, the five bachelor sons were Bill, Frank, John, Ed, and

Albert.[40] Don McAlavy in the *High Plains History* book, lists them as, "Bill, Frank, John, Bud, and Lewis."[41]

They established the T-41 Ranch near the springs at the northern end of the Tierra Blanca Lake and ran five hundred to one thousand cattle under the Backward Seven brand.

Their first house was a fourteen by twenty-five foot sod house consisting of a living room and kitchen. The boys had a twelve by twenty-four foot bunk house, also of sod. The corrals were made of barbed wire with a windbreak on the north side made out of soap weeds.[42]

As far as we know, they were not kin to Judge C. L. Carter or his offspring, Edna, Nelle, Byrd, and Lee Carter, who was a surveyor during the homestead period.

Potter knew the Carter family well and has said of them: "They were a real pioneer family. All of them smoked pipes, even to the Old Lady. They were a contented, happy family; the boys were nice to their mother, assisting her in every way."

Potter told of a tragic incident in the lives of the Carter sons: "There was a tragedy in the Carter family that I don't believe many people knew. Away back when the buffalo hunter was on the range, after a blizzard while the Carters were on the Agua Negro, four of the Carter boys went south to drift their cattle back.

"They were fifteen miles from home, and contacted a bunch of buffalo hunters on horseback. The Carters thought they were Indians and started back home as fast as they could go. The buffalo hunters were surprised and wanted to make a contact and followed them chasing them for several miles.

"One of the boys, Frank, in his early teens, let his horse become winded, and he got off and made the race on home on foot. He never got over the scare. Before he got grown, he would get scary spells and leave home. For about three years he would

---

[40] Jack Potter. letters to Rose White. 1940-1950.

[41] Harold Kilmer & Don McAlavy. *High Plains History*. (U.S.A.: High Plains Historical Press. 1980.) p. 40.

[42] Rose White. Article. *Portales Daily News*.

leave home at times and sometimes be tramping over the country for several months and then return home, and seemed to be all right.

"He had a nice little herd of cattle, a hundred or more. Finally about the year 1887, he left home with one of those scary spells and never did return. It was very sad for those old pioneer couple, pioneering out there when their hair was as white as the snow."

The Carters remained at Tierra Blanca about ten years and then moved and settled east of Amarillo. When the Carters left, the Tierra Blanca Ranch was taken over by the LFDs.

The lake has been dry for many years. Salt cedar bushes gradually took over and created a virtual forest on the white caliche flats left by the dried up lake bed. In the fifties, it was a favorite camping spot for scout troops. My husband Mike took his Troop 125 there many times to learn camping skills.

The Riley Family

The Riley family were also among the first ranchers forced out when the XIT purchased most of ten counties in the Texas Panhandle. They settled in the sandhills north of Portales Springs.

Potter was well-acquainted with the Rileys, and wrote about them in a letter to Rose White: "I do not know what part of the Plains they came from, but know that they came in to the Sandhills in the middle 1880s. The Rileys and their in-laws were a very peculiar set of people. Pioneers, ignorant in some ways, but proved to know how to 'cumilate'.

"There were several of the Riley sons. Their brand was their name, RILY. This brand went on all the Riley cattle. To designate the ownership among the family, they put the initial on the neck, T RILY for Tom Riley and B RILY for Boy Riley, and C RILY for Cage. The in-laws were Charly Moore, Clever Mason, Charly Callis and Billy Arrington.

"They were a happy family, but their cattle increased so fast that they run short of water, and the in-laws commenced migrating to newer fields. Charly Moore went to Idaho. Billy

Arrington, Charly Callis, and Clever Mason migrated to this part of the country. The other Rileys stayed in the sandhills.

"It seemed that Tom, the old bachelor, was the business one in the family. After the old folks died, he was the boss. To show you how peculiar they were, when Amarillo became a town and market and shipping point, the Riley people drove their steers to market, two or three years crop.

"Well they found a buyer from Woodward, Okla. and sold them and taken the buyer's check for six thousand dollars. They loaded their wagon down with supplies and went home.

"A good strong year had passed and the check never came in for payment. The buyer drew out the money, but he was an honest man; finally the check did come in, and the buyer dug up the money and taken it up.

"This is the way they done business. They were not used to money, only on a small scale. First the old folks died and several hundred cattle were divided among the in-laws. Then the old bachelor Tom died, and there was another division. I know the in-laws up here got quite a stake from the division."[43]

According to Potter, all the Rileys were not law-abiding: "Cage Riley was the youngest son and the black sheep of the family. He and Portales Bill were pals and they rustled cattle, stole horses and Riley was jailed several times.

"I have plenty to tell on the Rileys. I don't think they ever had a bedstead in their house for several years. Old Billy Arrington felt like taking something home for the old lady and family and bought an iron bedstead, mattress and springs. Well when he got home everything went well until bedtime.

"The bed was put in order, and the lady says, 'Bill, you ain't going to get me to sleep on that thing. I might fall off and break my neck.' So she spread the mattress down on the floor where she felt safer."

In an article in the Portales News-Tribune, Mrs. Della Riley described how she and her husband Bud lived and operated a blacksmith shop where the old First National Bank

---

[43] Potter.

stood at Second and Main in Portales. Their business was mostly shoeing horses and fixing buggy wheels.

Describing the town, she says: "There was nothing here but sand hills and saloons. There wasn't much here in 1900, and there was nothing at all in Clovis; not even the name.

"As a matter of fact, when the railroad finally was built through the present site of Clovis, it was called Riley's Switch, after my husband's brothers, Roy and Henry Riley, cowboys who operated from what is now the Bivens Ranch."[44]

However, Della and Bud Riley became discouraged with the lack of activity and the constant wind which even kept her from lighting a fire in the fireplace. Believing there was no future here, they moved their family to Texas.

Harold Kilmer and Don McAlavy have a good write-up on the Rileys in the book, *High Plains History,* available at all of the local libraries.[45]

Typical dugout home with Waller family. Harold Kilmer & Don McAlavy. *High Plains History Book.* 1980.

---

[44] Della Riley. Article. *Portales News-Tribune.* May 14, 1950.

[45] Kilmer. p.54.

Maj. George W. Littlefield. ENMU Golden Library Special
Collections

W.P. and Euphemia Littlefield family. Courtesy of Pat Boone IV.

Chapter 8
The LFD and the T-71 Ranches

The LFD and T-71 Ranches were originated by a family that still looms large in the history of the Llano Estacado. George W. Littlefield was born on a plantation in Mississippi, and came to Gonzales, Texas with his family at the age of nine. There he farmed until the Civil War broke out and at the age of nineteen, he volunteered for the army. He was promoted to major, but received a disabling wound at the battle of Mossy Creek which ended his military service.

Major Littlefield got his start in the cattle business in 1871 when he and brother W. P. and nephews Tom and Phelps White rounded-up a herd of long-horned cattle and drove them from the ranch at Gonzales, Texas to Dodge City, Kansas. He organized the LIT Ranch at Tascosa, Texas and remained there until 1881, when he sold out to the XIT and moved his operation to Bosque Grande on the Pecos River in New Mexico. This ranch was pioneered by John Chisum to feed the Indians who had been incarcerated at Ft. Sumner by the army.

Littlefield scoured Lousiana and bought thousands of dogies at a dollar and a half a head and double-decked them on the cars like sheep and hogs. He unloaded them in Texas, wintered them on the range, and in the spring sold four thousand of them to Phelps and Tom White at eight dollars a head, delivered at Bosque Grande.[46] His new brand was LFD for the beginning, middle, and last letters of the Littlefield name.

The ranches near the Pecos River had many of the same problems encountered by ranches to the east. However, unlike their neighbors on the east, they had a steady supply of water,

---

[46] J. Evetts Haley. *George W. LIttlefield Texan*. (Norman: University of Oklahoma Press. 1943) p. 137.

even though the river water was said to be almost too alkaline to drink, especially in a prolonged drought.

In addition they had quicksand and bogs, and cattle were constantly lost to drowning. Bog-riders were sent out on both sides of the river to drag out and tail-up cows caught along the marshy banks. Like all ranchers on the Llano, they had to contend with lobo wolves, rustlers, snow storms, prairie fires, and drifting cattle, along with the uncertainty of getting cattle to market.

According to a newspaper account, "Once a fire broke out on tthe LFD caattle lands and spread rapidly over the rank growth of grass, the wind driving the flame in a solid wall thirty feet high. The manager, Phelps White, with all the available help started for the scene of the fire and the most heroic work was done to turn the blaze but to no avail. Phelps had driven out to the wave of the fire in his mule team, and upon nearing it, the wind shifted the fire toward him. The team turned and ran away, and with the swift blaze gaining rapidly, the mules ran into a barbed wire fence. To run from the fire was useless, to face the blaze seemingly certain death. Phelps jumped from the buggy and broke into the fire of hell but fell down, his clothes catching fire. He started again but again fell down, each time from suffocation.

"He was carried to the ranch house and Dr. Pearce sent for. When Dr. Pearce reached the bedside, a most horrible piece of suffering humanity confronted him. First easing Phelp's intense pain, an examination revealed deep burns between the hips and slight burns down to and around his ankles where the tops of his boots were burned off. Although his hands received deep burns and one of his lips was burned to the bone, he will not be seriously scarred."[47]

In 1885 Littlefield's trusted trail boss Charles S. McCarty was encouraged to establish a ranch near a hidden spring just north of the present town of Kenna. He bought out the Hernandez Brothers who had a horse ranch near a grove of chinaberry and hackberry trees. McCarty brought his bride Sallie

---

[47] Article. *Portales Times.* April 2, 1904.

to the new adobe home which they named T 71, and this became the brand on their cattle.

The nearest post office to the T 71 was Roswell, fifty miles away. Most of the groceries were freighted from Amarillo, Texas, 160 miles to the northeast. Large herds would be driven to Amarillo to be shipped by rail to market. Groceries and supplies would be brought back, the round trip requiring several weeks. The stagecoach traveled from Amarillo to Roswell, 1865 to 1905, passing by the T 71 Ranch. The few ranch houses would be the only sign of civilization for miles around. The equipment of the stage companies, as well as the unpredictable traveling conditions, could usually assure the traveler of many hours of discomfort. [48]

McCarty sold his interest at the T 71 to J. P. White, T. D. Whte and George W. Littlefield of the Littlefield Cattle Company in 1896. Later Joe Wilcox purchased the T 71 and he and his family lived there for many years.

Maj. Littlefield ranched several years at Bosque Grande, but soon found out why Charles Goodnight had called the Pecos "the graveyard of a cowman's hopes." The rainfall was undependable and in a drought year, the water in the Pecos dried up and left puddles of gyppy water that became so alkaline it could kill man or beast. On one drive, several hands drank from a hole of stagnant water that caused every man to lose all the hair from his head. Some outfits carried canned tomatoes or vinegar and soda as relief from the Pecos water.

As the cattle searched for water, they often got bogged down in the banks of the Pecos. "All up and down its glistening, gyppy course, every cowboy was riding bog, 'tromping' the hardened sand into a quicky condition about each mired cow and then pulling her out by the horn of his saddle. Then he would tail the weakened animal up and start it on its tottering way. It was man killing work."[49]

In 1886 Littlefield moved his cattle to the undeveloped Four-Lakes area in what is now Lea County. Littlefield had a

---

[48] Jayne Wilcox Taylor. *Kenna, a Ranching Community.* (Elida: 1991.) p. 2.

[49] Haley. p. 153.

sharp head for business and over the years was involved in numerous endeavors including several ranches, banks, and other businesses in Texas and New Mexico. It was his habit to assist employees and relatives in starting ranches close by his, thus assuring himself of friendly neighbors. He involved his large family in various enterprises and was said to have put twenty-nine relatives through the University of Texas and helped them get a start in business. The town of Littlefield is named for him.

Littlefield's brother William P. "Bill" elected to stay on the Llano. He and wife Euphemia K. Mathieu had come to work at Bosque Grande, but in 1883 when W. P. was traveling from the Pecos ranch, he came upon a hidden spring on Kenna Mesa and decided to locate a ranch there. The spring had been known to Indian hunting parties for many years, but they kept it covered with rocks and branches to hide it from buffalo hunters and settlers.

W. P. enlarged the spring and built a house close by. It was said that four adobe brick-makers were brought in from Mexico to do the principle work on the building, and the lumber and the hardware for the house were brought in by ox-drawn wagons from Las Vegas, New Mexico. The old ranch house was still being used up until the year two thousand by descendants of the family.

W.P. loved the isolation of the ranch, but his fondness of solitude was not shared by his wife, Euphemia. She hired a Negro family to help with the chores, and a governess to take care of the five daughters and one son, and to teach them their lessons.

Patrick Henry Boone came to the Llano Estacado from the family home in Missouri after his father died of Bright's disease. According to Patrick Henry Boone III, "When my grandfather Boone turned eighteen years of age in 1871, he told his mother that he intended to leave Missouri and go out into the world to seek his fortune. He left and went out to settle in Eastern New Mexico west of Portales Springs on what is listed on the old maps as 'Boone Draw.'

"He got in the cattle business very early, running little bunches of cattle and horses on the public domain, and at one time I think ran cattle over in the neighbothood of Billy the Kid Spring over on the northwest end of our [present] ranch."[50]

When he and Mildred Littlefield, daugter of W. P. and Euphemia, were married in 1890, they combined their ranges and later went to live in the old W. P. Littlefield home.

Mildred had a pet antelope that she raised from a baby which followed her around like a puppy. She tied a red silk satin bow around its neck to protect it from hunters. When she and Mr. Boone left for Roswell in a buggy after being married, the antelope followed them and was never seen again.

Boone raised both horses and cattle, but was fondest of his prize horses. The story was told that once when a circus came to the little town of Roswell, he took his mare to the circus grounds. She happened to be in heat and he bribed an animal handler there with a fifty cent piece to carry the mare in to be bred to a fine Arabian stallion owned by the circus. The resulting colt, Popcorn, was the father of many fine horses.

Descendants of the Boone family have continued to ranch at the same location up until the present time

T 71 Ranch house. Old postcard. Courtesy Jayne Wilcox Taylor.

---

[50] Patrick H. Boone III. *An Oral History.* Dictated December 1986. LIttlefield, Texas. Courtesy of Pat Boone IV.

Jim Newman

Jim Newman. Burns Collection.

Chapter 10
Jim Newman of the DZ

James F. "Jim" Newman had come to Texas from Arkansas, and in 1879 he moved his herd from Navarro County to a ranch in Nolan and Fisher Counties near Sweetwater. In 1881 he bought the water rights to George Causey's buffalo camp at Yellow House and located his cattle there.

Yellow House, near the present site of Littlefield, fell inside the XIT property; so in 1882 Newman had to begin moving his 2,700 cattle to Salt Lake, now Grulla Wildlife Refuge, just across the state line in New Mexico. Since his brand was "DZ," the ranch was known by that name.

With him came several cowhands, including Sid Boykin, Walter Fulcher, Julius Darby, a black man, and my step-grandfather, R. L. "Bob" Wood, who was Newman's first cousin. Jim had bought the rights to the water from Andy McDonald. Andy's brother Will was also at the ranch, and Will's wife, Lizzie, became camp cook.[51]

Dan McFatter, DZ cowhand, described the ranch, "The men dug troughs at the northeastern end of Salt Lake to catch the spring water which flowed into the lake, and built an adobe house. The roof was of sod, supported by heavy beams. I have heard Jim complain that the beams cost him $10 apiece, by the time they were cut and freighted from Las Vegas. The roof would not leak the day it rained, but two or three days later, the water would begin to soak through."[52]

---

[51] R. L. Wood. interview by Rose White. 1932.

[52] Dan McFatter. interview with Rose White. 1949.

A person could only legally own forty acres where his water and dwelling were located. However, it was the custom for each rancher to claim the thousands of acres where he ran his cattle. According to Bob Wood, "The DZ claimed all the territory to the Canadian river on the north, to the Pecos river on the west, forty miles south to the Four Lakes, the line of the LFD Ranch, and to the Texas line on the east."

There were no fences except drift fences which were constructed to keep the cattle from drifting in bad weather. It was against the law to build fences, so when it was rumoured that an inspector was in the vicinity, the fences were hurriedly taken down. Half-dugout line camps were set up at various points along the perimeter of the ranch for the men keeping an eye on the cattle. They would "ride the line" between these dugouts to find and turn back any cattle that had strayed.

My grandmother, Ora Wood, has said that Jim Newman was like a character out of a western novel. "He was part Cherokee Indian, was dark and heavy-set with a black mustache. He had a quick temper and at various times, would fire all the cowboys and later hire them back when he had cooled off."[53]

Dan McFatter told of one incident when Newman was more agreeable: "Once Jim Newman took a notion he wanted a desk at the DZ to keep his papers in. We built it in the yard; was awful proud of it till we found it was too big to go through the door. When Jim come, he says, 'Hell! I'll use it out here!'"

Newman could be generous, said McFatter: "There was a negro named Snow working on the place and Jim Newman had given him two or three calves. At the time I am telling you about they had increased till he had six or seven head under his own brand. The cook at that time was a Mexican, and he and Snow got into an argument which ended by Snow killing the Mexican and running away. We buried the Mexican by Salt Lake. Jim afterwards bought Snow's cattle from his mother at Colorado City."

Newman was a great talker and would entertain the cowhands for hours with his tales of wild adventures. He could

---

53 Ora Wood. Interview by Rose White.1935.

ride any horse on the ranch and raised champion race horses back in Texas. He maintained his home in Sweetwater, and was sheriff of Nolan County for many years.

Bob Wood related, "One of the stories I have always enjoyed is the one about Jim Newman. You see, he was shot in the back by an enemy, said to be Dick English, one time. It didn't kill him, but he went clear to New York City to have the slugs dug out of his back. He saved them, and the cowboys swore that the same slugs were used to kill the enemy. The man was waylaid and killed at Sweetwater, but no one was ever convicted of his murder."

Doak Good had settled in comfortably in his rock and adobe house at Portales Springs, but his peaceful existence did not last long. His trouble with Jim Newman started soon after Newman arrived at Salt Lake. When Newman began bringing his cattle from Texas to Salt Lake and established the DZ Ranch, it was only eleven miles east of Good's place. The springs that fed Salt Lake only provided enough water to fill a few dirt troughs, so the DZ cattle would drift over to the plentiful water at the lake which was fed by the Portales Springs.

Jack Potter said, "When Newman was crowded out of Yellow House XIT pasture and established the ranch at Salt Lake with hardly any water, only enough for about fifty steers, he did not seem to want any stock water while his neighbors had plenty for all hands."[54]

This situation was bound to cause trouble and violence soon erupted between Newman and Doak Good. After the fight with Gabe Henson, which he blamed on Newman, Good was afraid to stay by himself and he picked up a transient boy about fourteen years old to work for him.

Jack Potter had this to say about the new cowhand, "He was a hard-looking kid; had an old Stetson hat with the crown out, thrown away by some cowpuncher. He had long hair and it stuck out through the crown of the hat. He was dubbed by the cowboys as 'Portales Bill,' though I learned later his real name was McElmore.

_____

54 Jack Potter.letters to Rose White. 1940-1950.

"Good gave him a few dogies or mavericks for his work, and it was commonly believed that he added to his herd by rustling other people's cattle.

"A 'dogie' is a calf that has lost its mother and a 'maverick' is a full-grown animal that has somehow escaped being branded. It was the accepted custom that all dogies and mavericks belonged to the man on whose range they were found. However, many a cowman added to his herd by branding any unmarked cattle, no matter on whose range they were found.

"Not only did outlaws brand mavericks on another rancher's land, they would also deface brands already on the cattle. With a running iron, a branding iron with only a single bar on it, it was fairly easy to change a brand to another mark entirely.

"One day at a roundup over on Newman's range, Newman's men told the kid that they claimed any fresh-branded mavericks on their range. The kid bawled them out, pulled a gun, rode into the roundup, cut out the cattle he had branded and took them home. No one was inclined to stop him, even though they were sure the cattle belonged to the DZ.

"After leaving Good's ranch, Portales Bill went from bad to worse. He became pals with Cage Riley, who was said to be the black sheep of the Riley family who had settled in the sandhills to the north. Together, they were involved in scrapes involving stolen cattle and horses and were jailed several times.

"Portales Bill joined up with the bunch of rustlers who were operating around the Tucumcari area and was involved with the group who were stealing XIT cattle near Mesa Redondo, fifteen to twenty miles south of Tucumcari.

"A posse of lawmen and ranchers surprised the gang at Mesa Redondo and killed several suspected rustlers. Portales Bill was surrounded at the Francisco de Baca ranch near Endee, New Mexico, and when he refused to surrender, the posse killed him. He is buried in the Old Endee cemetery."

When Jim Newman came back from a trip east, he brought with him a reputed bad man named Harry Blocker. At one time foreman for Newman, Blocker was considered a bad man by many, but was liked by the cowmen, remembered Joe Beasley.[55]

According to Dan McFatter, "Blocker knew little or nothing about a cow, but Jim put him in charge of the outfit. Dressed like a movie cowboy, he strutted around in a big hat, fancy vest, and two guns. Not good at riding or roping, there was one thing he could do; he was quick on the draw.

"Harry Blocker was a no-good horse thief. Several times, some fine horses arrived at the DZ. Nobody seemed to know who they belonged to, and no one claimed them. But, in a few days, Blocker would disappear with the horses, and come back with money in his pockets. Once he ended up in jail in East Texas and how he got out of that scrape, I don't know."

"Harry Blocker was nothing but a hoss thief," agreed Col. Potter.

Disillusioned and tired of all the fighting, out-manned and out-gunned by the larger ranch, Good finally sold out his claim and left the country, complaining bitterly that Newman had crowded him out.

Newman continued to increase his herd up to ten thousand head until 1894 when he sold the DZ rights to W. R. "Bill" Curtis of the Diamond Tail Ranch in Texas. Then Newman and his brother-in-law, Tom Trammell, bought the H-Bar Ranch from Dr. Caleb Winfrey.[56]

---

[55] Joe Beasley. Interview by Rose White.1937.

[56] Wood.

Chapter 11
DZ Mac

Dan R. McFatter was one of the well-known cowboys who worked for Jim Newman at the DZ Ranch for many years. He also worked for Doak Good for a time when Jim fired him in a fit of rage. Jim would often lose his temper and fire one of the men and then hire him back when his temper cooled.

Mr. McFatter was an unusual man, clear and concise in his memories and never one to brag about his exploits. When he told a story that showed him up in a favorable light, it was never his skill or perseverance or daring that caused him to win out. Always, he attributed his success to good luck, or to the help of friends, or to sheer accident.[57] Dan McFatter was born in central Mississippi in 1855. This made him ten years old when the Civil War ended. He remembered hearing the cannons firing a long way off, but said the fighting never came near his home. His father had volunteered at the beginning of the War, but after a few months of fighting, he contracted measles and was sent home. Unfortunately, he had been wet and cold, and this "drove the measles in on him" and he died.

Like many other boys, Dan grew up with a stronger and stronger desire to be a cowboy. Finally he could stand it no longer. He told his mother and brothers and sisters good-bye and took the train for Hico, Texas. His reason for going there was this: At Hico lived the Oldhams, friends of the McFatter family and distantly related as fifth or sixth cousins of the McFatters.

At Hico he was given work by Mr. Oldham at his livery stable. Between trips West he would return to Hico, always sure of a job and a welcome. Mr. W. B. Oldham, then a small child,

---

[57]Dan McFatter. interview by Rose White. 1939.

later a successful business man in Portales, has told how much the Oldham children thought of the tall, friendly cowboy, always called by them, "Mr. Dan."

Said Mr. Oldham, "He was my boyhood hero. He was fond of children and he entertained us with exciting tales of his adventures. I kept begging him for a wild mustang pony. My mother was afraid it would hurt me, and she gave him strict orders not to bring it to me. Every time he would come back, I would ask for my bronco. If I live to be a hundred, I will never get over my disappointment because I never got it."

McFatter worked for various ranches for several years before he went to work for the DZ Ranch in the fall of 1885. He worked there until 1891 when he went to work for Doak Good at Portales Springs. He also worked for Doc Winfrey at the H-Bar Ranch before it was sold to Newman.

McFatter told of his time at the DZ, "In the time I worked for Jim Newman, we drove our cattle to Colorado City to be shipped. There were antelope in droves on the plains. They would stay in herds in winter, then go off in pairs in the spring. The XIT had a rule that no one could kill an antelope. They got as gentle as lambs.

"There were lots of coyotes and wolves, and they took a heavy toll in calves. The Government had a premium on their heads, but the cowboys never bothered to shoot them.

"Twelve or fifteen cowboys were used with a trail herd. Five or six stayed at the DZ Ranch in summer, only one or two in winter. Two winters I stayed all alone at the DZ. The house ran east and west. The east end was a half-dugout against the bluff. One evening, a dreadful storm came up out of the northeast. It snowed and blew all night. Next morning, I opened the east door and found it blocked by a solid wall of snow. But the west door was clear. I didn't clear the snow away, just used the other door till the snow melted.

"I didn't mind it much, but in the spring I would get anxious for the freighters' wagons to come. With a telescope, I would watch the hill, three miles away. When they finally did come in sight, I would saddle my horse and gallop out to meet them. How glad I was to see some people again! They would bring me magazines and papers, and tell me the news of the outside world."

There was always tension between the cattlemen and the sheepmen. The ranchers claimed that the sheep ruined the land for cattle by grazing the grass off so short that it didn't grow back.

McFatter told of one friendly encounter with a neighboring sheepman: "For a while, one Foster, brother-in-law of Eiland, ran 2500 sheep south of the DZ. In hard northers, the sheep would drift south. We had a floating outfit; a four-mule team and wagon with food and four barrels of water. We would stay out till we used up the water. We had to have water, not only for ourselves, but also for the horses. After one bad storm, we started out to round up the badly drifted cattle. We had been out one and one-half days when, one morning, I got breakfast, then started out to find the cattle.

"I had come forty or forty-five miles from the DZ headquarters when, on coming over a rise, I saw what looked like a whole valley full of sheep. I rode back to the wagon and asked Jim Stone, 'Would you know old Foster's sheep?' Jim says, 'Yes, sure, I'd know that old bell sheep anywhere.' I said, 'Come on. See if these sheep are Foster's.'

"We went back, and sure enough, Jim said they was Foster's sheep. We drove them back to camp. I changed horses, drove the sheep all night, and next morning till ten o'clock. I got the sheep to the foot of some hills, then rode on to Foster's house. When I told him I had the sheep, he was the proudest man you ever saw. He had such bad eyesight, he was nearly blind.

"He gave me some breakfast. I wanted to be getting some sleep; but he says, 'Mac, I couldn't find those sheep in a thousand years. You just got to go with me and show me where they are.'

"Well, I went with him and brought them on in. On the way in, he says, 'Mac, there is a mortgage on those sheep. The first storm that comes, they'll drift again, and you know I can't trail 'em worth a cent. If you'll stay and he'p me, I'll give you a half-interest in the sheep.'

"The old man begged and pleaded, but I told him I wasn't interested. All I wanted was some sleep. I fell into his bed, and slept till sundown. I wasn't no sheep man, and didn't want to be one."

McFatter bought a ranch at Canadian, Texas, and lived there until shortly before his death on February 14, 1952 at age 95.

Half-dugout. Burns collelction.

Jim Stone. Cowboy Banker. Courtesy David Stone.

Chapter 12
Jim Stone: Cowboy Banker

James Polk "Jim" Stone was another of the cowboys who worked at the DZ Ranch when it was moved across the New Mexico border from Texas.

He was born in 1868 in Limestone County, Texas, and migrated with his family to Brown County. In 1888 he and his two brothers, Andrew and Will, established a ranch south of Doak Good at Portales Springs. His brand was "S inside a diamond."

Stone was of a quiet nature and didn't take part in some of the more adventurous activities of the cowboys. At one time he had an adobe house above the Sid Boykin's place on Running Water Draw, and Lizzie Boykin has said of him: "The cowboys used to say that when Jim Stone went to town, he would not get drunk, as the others did, but would buy him a sack of candy and go back to the wagon to eat it. Maybe those quiet habits helped him to become a rich man before he died."[58]

When Jim worked for the DZ Ranch at Salt Lake he was well-liked by the other cowboys. He was a champion steer roper and continued to compete in ropings up until he was 38 years old.

At that time, there were no roping pens, only chutes, so once turned loose, the steers ran until they were taken down. At one roping, Jim broke three ropes trying to rope a difficult steer. When the third rope broke, he threw it down and declared he was through roping steers.

Jim and Lula Beasley were married in 1898 and she was later one of the first women elected to the Portales school board. When Jim became involved in the banking business, she served

---

[58] Lizzie Boykin. interview by Rose White. 1949.

as a director. She and Mr. Stone helped organize the First Methodist Church in Portales.

In 1900, with the homesteaders pouring in on the new railroad, Jim saw a need for a bank. People did not have much money, but after the sale of a herd of cattle there would be large sums of gold and paper money to contend with. Also, many of the homesteaders had sold everything they owned before traveling to their new claims and needed a place to safely store the proceeds until it could be used for building materials and livestock.

Stone established the Bank of Portales in the new little town that had sprung up near the depot. It was the first brick building in the town and was located on south Main. The building still stands today, next to the Portales News-Tribune. The bank was later named the Citizen's Bank of Portales.

Jim opened the First National Bank of Elida in 1906. It was later moved to Portales by his son Doug; and it still operates as the James Polk Stone Community Bank on Second Street under the direction of Jim's grandson, David L. Stone. Stone, Justin Click, T. E. Mears and Graham Bryant were also involved in establishing banks at Texico, Ft. Sumner, and Hereford, Texas.

The banking business in the early days on the High Plains was as wild and unpredictable as the other occupations of the time. The bank at Elida holds the distinction of being the only bank in the area ever held up by armed bandits. In 1928 three outlaws invaded the bank, secured the employees in the vault and made off with the cash. They then fled in an easterly direction, hotly pursued by the sheriff. They ran out of gas near Arch, but made it by hitchhiking to Amarillo, Texas where they were arrested.

In one incident, the notorious gunman, Jim Miller, was outsmarted by the quick thinking and ingenuity on the part of Stone. Miller was widely known as being an outlaw who killed for hire and was suspected of being the murderer of Pat Garrett. He was eventually lynched in Oklahoma for killing a Federal Marshal.

Jack Potter wrote, "In regard to Jim Miller, he killed people for so much per head. He belonged west of the Pecos in the Guadalupe Mountains and the Tulerosa country. Some early day people think that he killed Pat Garrett. Miller and Oliver Lee were friends, and Garrett was petitioned to come back from Texas and run down the murderers of Col. Fountain. This was done by Dona Ana County, and Garrett had Oliver Lee arrested but could not prove anything.

"After Garrett was killed a very few days afterwards, Jim Miller made a deal with some people at Ada, Oklahoma to kill a certain prominent man. The man lived long enough to tell who done the killing, so the people of Ada, rounded up Miller and his two pals and hung them in a livery stable in Ada. I have heard people say that the time was so short after the killing of Garrett that he must of rode to Ada, Okla in relays, the time was so short."[59]

Miller had made a deal with the Eiland Brothers, who ran a flock of sheep south of Portales Springs, to trade a piece of land in south Texas for the sheep. He hired a local young man to herd the sheep to the railhead for shipment to Kansas City.

The problem was that Stone's bank had a mortgage for $3,500 on the sheep. Banker Stone, knowing that Miller was a crook, tried to stop the trade, but the sheep were already across the Texas line. Stone quickly took up the mortgage, jumped on a train north and intercepted the sheep in Kansas City.

There he recovered the $3,500. The poor Eiland brothers were left with the worthless land in Texas, but Stone escaped without harm.[60]

Jim Stone died in 1913 and is buried with his wife in the Portales Cemetery. One of the few family-owned businesses that has survived from 1900 to the present, the James Polk Stone Banks now include banks in Portales, Clovis, Roswell, Hagerman, Hobbs, and a website for internet banking.[61]

---

[59] Jack Potter. letter to Rose White. May 25, 1949.

[60] Article. "Jim Miler, 'Meanest Man in West' Figured in Swindle Here." Portales News-Tribune. September 21, 1952.

[61] David Stone. interview by Ruth Burns. 2009.

"Ghost Steer." Drawing by Pat Burns.

Chapter 13
Bob Wood and the Ghost Steer

The story of my grandfather R. L. "Bob" Wood differs somewhat from that of the ordinary cowboy. The rough and tumble cowboy of the 1800s was not much inclined to superstitions: ghosts, demons, spirits, or haunts. He did not worry much about supernatural beings, but occasionally some old-timer might be visited by a "haint" or the spirit of a long-lost companion. Ordinarily, cowhands were too caught up in the hard work and unending challenges of tending a herd of cows to be worried about apparitions.

Now in order to be a true ghost story, the ghost must be real, not a case of mistaken identity, but a true messenger from another world of animate beings. The ghost in this story was of this latter kind: a true supernatural manifestation sent to give a message to a particular person. The cowboy in this story believed in the ghost implicitly; so much so that he followed the ghost's advice; so much so that these messages shaped the course of his whole career. This cowboy was my grandfather, Bob Wood.

Wood was born in Navarro County, Texas, in 1864, just at the close of the Civil War. His parents were poor, but so was everyone in Texas, so it didn't seem too bad. When he was very small both his father and his mother died and he was taken into the family of an aunt. Her husband was a hardheaded man who beat his own and his foster children unmercifully.

Bob never advanced beyond the third grade in school and so could just barely read and write. He could sign his name, but didn't try to write a letter. However he could work out any problem involving arithmetic in his head. He could figure the number of cattle to be sold and the total price and would practically never make a mistake.

When Bob was twelve years old he revolted against the cruelty of his uncle and left home. By then he was a tall, strong lad, made tough by hard work and spare living. Bob packed up his few belongings and left, never to return.

Though he was only twelve he got a job as a farmhand at fifteen dollars a month with room and board. After three months, when Bob asked for his pay, he was told, "Well, I had to deduct for your laundry, and for horse feed, and the loan of a hoe and a rake. I figure you owe me fifty cents."

A man named Wolfe happened to overhear the conversation and offered him a job helping drive a trail herd to Dodge City, Kansas. Bob jumped at the chance.

This was the boy's first experience as a cowboy. He loved the outdoor work, the horses and the cattle and the association with men who treated him like an equal. The working with cattle was to be his chosen occupation, and he loved it to the end of his life. Though he farmed a little in his later years he cared nothing about it, and he had the cowboy's traditional contempt for chickens or sheep, and an abhorrence for the idea of milking a cow.

At seventeen he made his first trip West. It was to be the first of many journeys to New Mexico and it gave him his first glimpse of the land that was to become his permanent home. A man referred to as "Old Man Douthitt" wanted to hire Bob to help move the Boot-Bar cattle to the Guadelupe Mountains. Bob has told that he wasn't sure he wanted to go. This is his story in his own words:

"The night before we was to start, I was still trying to make my mind up to go. Hit was a bright moonlight night, and I was a-settin' out near the corrals. All of a sudden, I heerd a steer bawling. Hit warn't the ordinary sound a steer makes; hit was a most peculiar, bell-like note. I looked in the direction the sound come from, and I saw this steer a-standing on this little rise in the moonlight, calling to me. Often after, I saw him when I was planning a move. Always he called in the same way, and always he told me to move futher West."[62]

---

[62] Bob Wood. interview by Rose White. 1932.

Following the advice of the Ghost Steer, Bob went with Old Man Douthitt to move the cattle. The next year, 1882, he was offered a permanent job by his cousin, Jim Newman, who was starting a new ranch at Salt Lake in what is now Roosevelt County, New Mexico. As Bob debated the decision to move to New Mexico, the Ghost Steer appeared; and with its lonely cry, it again advised him to move West.

Bob worked at the DZ Ranch for many years. Dan McFatter said of him: "I worked right with Bob Wood all of the six years I was with Jim at the DZ. He was always jolly and good-hearted, a friend to everybody; but he was all business too. The men was always quarreling about night guard. No one ever wanted the middle watch, because that meant they would have to dress and undress twicet. But they all wanted the last watch, just before day, because then they would just get up early and stay up.

"But Bob would arrange it peaceable and have all satisfied. He'd joke them out of their bad humor and arrange things the way he wanted them. He was wagon boss a good part of the time when I was there. The men always got along good when he was in charge, but usually they was quarreling and grouchy all the time."

However, young Bob did get in trouble once, according to McFatter: "I felt so bad about the trouble Bob got in with Harry Blocker. I kept telling him that Harry was no good, but he wouldn't listen. Harry was always playing some prank, and that just suited Bob. I didn't trust Blocker; too many shady things happened when he was around.

"For instance, one time a stranger brought two beautiful cream-colored horses to the DZ; the prettiest matched pair of hosses you ever see. When he went on, he left those hosses. They stayed in a little pasture east of the house. Harry Blocker tended to them himself, would not let no one go near them. Then one day he made some excuse to leave the ranch and the hosses went with him. Of course he came back without them, but with more money than usual.

"I reminded Bob of all this, but he was so wropt up in Harry, he could not see it. Well, they went off together and they ended up in trouble in Sweetwater, Texas, just as I knew they would. I don't know how they got out of jail. I guess Newman went and bailed them out."[63]

After fifteen years, Newman sold the DZ Ranch, and moved his cattle to the H-Bar Ranch twenty miles to the west of Salt Lake. He offered Bob Wood the job of foreman.

At this time, Bob was thirty-three years old. He proposed to a young widow, Mrs. R. E. "Ora" White, of Sweetwater, Texas, who had two small sons, Eddie and Bill. She proved to be willing, and they prepared to move their belongings to the new home. Again the Ghost Steer gave his approval of the move by bawling with his peculiar bell-like voice.

After four years at the H-Bar, Bob and Ora debated moving to a claim of their own, wanting to get the boys closer to the new little school in Portales. They did move to a farm west of town, again with the ghostly advice of Bob's friend the Ghost Steer, calling from a little rise to the West.

When I knew my grandfather in the 1930s, he was in his sixties and his black hair had turned to gray. He wore an old black hat, black pants and jacket, and a six-inch wide belt which in his words, "keeps my stummick from falling in." Like most old cowboys, the long years in the saddle, braving the cold of winter and heat of summer, had left him badly crippled with arthritis. He and Grandmother Ora lived next door to us, and he kept a little black coffee pot on the old iron stove twenty-four hours a day. The coffee was black and rank and scalding hot, and no one else could drink it, but he said it "kep' him goin'" and reminded him of the old days on the ranch.

Bob was a farmer for the rest of his life. He was never entirely happy with it, and always kept a few cattle in a lonely pasture to remind him of the glorious days of the free range and the free way of life, unhampered by the demands of civilization. He never moved again, and so had no more advice from the Ghost Steer.

Now, whether one believes this story or not doesn't greatly matter. The point is that Bob Wood believed it. He insisted

---

[63] Dan McFatter. interview by Rose White.1939.

that it was a ghost, and not an ordinary steer. It was definitely a messenger sent from heaven to tell a poor worried cowboy what was best to do. The fact that the messages were brought by a steer is also understandable: Bob Wood knew steers a lot better than he knew people, and he would be more likely to listen to a steer than he would to a ghostly man.

I have often wondered whether, when Mr. Wood died, just at dawn in 1934, if he heard the voice of the Ghost Steer calling him home. If he did so, it would have stood on a Western hill silhouetted against the morning sky, and its bell-like voice would have rung out clear and sweet on the still air. I have often imagined the Ghost Steer calling for the last time, and then fading away into the "Faraway Ranch of the Boss in the Sky."[64]

Ghost Steer[65]
by Mike Burns Jr.

Headin' west, always west
Following that steer, looking for good grass and fresh
    water
Across Texas----Sweetwater, Yellow House; then into the
    Yarner
Working for the DZ and the H-Bar
I know that Ghost Steer is here somewhere
He wants me to follow, but I say no
The white porches are my home now, no more riding
    west
Barbed wire and windmills mean I can stay
Sweet Ora, Bob and Bill; time to settle with a job to fill
Ghost Steer, find another cowboy
Lead him west
I'm done riding herd, eating dust, saving dogies
And following your trail
Adios, amigo

---

64 Rose White. "The Ghost Steer." Speech to New Mexico Folklore Society. 1948.

65 Mike Burns Jr. Poem. 2000.

Sid Boykin. Courtesy ENMU Golden Library Special Collections

Chapter 14
Sid and Lizzie Boykin

Sid Boykin was one of the cowboys of the early days on the Llano Estacado who made the successful move from the ranch to the business world.

According to Jack Potter, "Sid made his first trip to New Mexico in 1881 with Old Man George Taylor, when Taylor moved the Boot-Bar cattle from Texas. They arrived in December at the Hondo and turned the cattle loose with Jimmy Sutherland's herd. Sid went back to Sweetwater and stayed that winter and then came with Jim Newman to the DZ Ranch in the spring of 1882."[66]

Sid worked for the DZ until 1892 and then started in business for himself on a little spread southeast of Portales. Most cattlemen settled wherever there was room, without the formality of legal papers, but Sid filed on his place. He ran about three hundred cattle under the "SW" brand and did most of the work himself. His brother Frank "Babe" lived with Sid until 1897 when Babe married and moved to a place near the sandhills.[67]

Elizabeth "Lizzie" Boykin was one of the first women to come to the eastern plains. She had been raised Lizzie Walters down near the Ruidoso River where she had been a spectator to the Lincoln County War.

She remembered participants on both sides of the conflict, including Billy the Kid, as they often stopped at the Walters' home for a meal. Her father, along with many of the more peaceable settlers along the Hondo, did not wish to take sides in the dispute, as they had friends on both sides.

---

[66] Jack Potter. letter to Rose White..December 7, 1940.

[67] Lizzie Boykin. interview by Rose White.1940.

She later married Will McDonald and moved with him and his brother Andy to a ranch at Salt Lake in eastern New Mexico.

Joe Beasley said, "I knew Mrs. Sid Boykin when she was living with McDonald over on the Pecos. Her name was McDonald then. Her father's name was Walters. He ranched down past Alamogordo."[68]

Potter and Dan McFatter both agree that Lizzie McDonald was living at the DZ and working as a cook when Newman bought the rights at the DZ from Andy McDonald, brother of her husband Will.

Now that all persons involved are dead and gone, perhaps it will not hurt to speak of the situation in which these participants found themselves, according to both Potter and McFatter.

Dan McFatter said: "Mrs. Lizzie Boykin came to the DZ Ranch as a cook. Her husband's name was McDonald. He worked there too. Well, Lizzie struck up a love affair with Sid Boykin and left McDonald; later married Sid."[69]

In about 1896 Jim Newman fired my step-grandfather, Bob Wood, from the DZ, as he did every so often. Bob went and lived with Sid and Lizzie until Newman relented and hired him back. Bob always spoke kindly of Mrs. Boykin's hospitality and her good cooking.[70]

At a time when most ranches had no milk or butter, Sid always kept a milk cow at the house. Mrs. Sid kept chickens and had a nice little vegetable garden. In those days there were no crops in the country at all except for those at Sid's and at the H-Bar.

In 1898 Sid built a bigger house, but he only lived in it two and one-half years. When people began crowding in with the coming of the railroad, Sid wasn't satisfied. He moved his cattle south of Tucumcari and soon bought the ranch on the Frio Draw

---

[68] Joe Beasley. interview by Rose White. 1936.

[69] Dan McFatter. interview by Rose White. 1942.

[70] Bob Wood. interview by Rose White. 1930.

near the DeOliveira and Rhea families. He and Lizzie lived in a dugout for several years and then built a nice rock house.

Sid prospered in the cattle business and in 1913 he bought into the First National Bank of Clovis. In 1915 he, along with A. W. Skarda and S. A. Jones, bought controlling interest in the bank.

Sid and Lizzie built a house at 400 Sheldon Street in Clovis which still stands today. My mother Rose White was a frequent visitor in their home where Lizzie was known for her hospitality and her delicious coconut cakes.

Sid never lost his love of ranching and still owned the ranch on the Frio at the time of his death. He passed away in 1933 and Mrs. Boykin in 1952.[71]

MRS. S. J. BOYKIN

Lizzie Boykin. Clovis News-Journal.

---

[71] Harold Kilmer & Don McAlavy. "Sid Boykin." (U.S.A.: *High Plains History Book*. 1980.) p. 52.

H-Bar Ranch House. Water color by Rose White.

Chapter 15
The Winfreys at the H-Bar

In the early days before the coming of the railroad, the H-Bar Ranch was the ranch located nearest the future sites of Clovis and Portales. The H-Bar, situated where the Portales Country Club now stands, was established by some unlikely cowmen, and was associated with some wild characters in its early days.

It was 1884, just sixteen years after the end of the Civil War and three years after the death of Billy the Kid, that a group of Missourians traveled west to become cattle ranchers on the Llano Estacado.

These compadres from Cass County, Missouri, were W. G. Urton, J. D. Cooley, Lee Easley and others. They formed the Cass Land and Cattle Company and set up their operation on the Pecos River at Cedar Canyon, sixty miles northeast of the present site of Roswell.[72]

With them came a close acquaintance, Dr. Hadley Winfrey. Hadley had been sent to the Pecos country by his brother, Dr. Caleb Winfrey, who had decided to move to the Southwest in search of a more healthy climate. So in 1884 Hadley went ahead with his fellow Missourians to gather up a herd and find a suitable location for a ranch.

Jack Potter knew the Winfreys well. He worked on the roundup spring and summer with Hadley Winfrey throughout the Pecos roundups, when Hadley was gathering the cattle to move to the plains.

According to Potter, Dr. Caleb Winfrey was a peculiar man, ". . . kind of a curiosity; not like western men. He was highly educated and once told me that the country starting from the Tu-

---

[72] Cooley Urton. interview by Rose White. 1949.

les [near Melrose] on to Tierra Blanca, Portales Lake and on south was once a river, now covered up."[73] This area was later recognized as Black Water Draw and the old Brazos River.

Not typical cowmen, Winfrey and his bachelor brother Hadley had both been medical doctors in Kansas City, Missouri. Dr. Caleb had been a surgeon during the Civil War and was recognized for heroic action in the battle of Lone Jack Hill and other encounters.[74]

Hadley acquired about two thousand heifers at Ft. Griffin, Texas, and ranged them with the Cass Company herd. According to Potter, "In 1885 Dr. Winfrey and his family showed up at Fort Sumner and they prowled the whole country looking for a location so they could keep their herd intact."

With them came several cow hands and a Negro helper, known only as "the Winfrey Negro." Col. Potter has said that Dr. Winfrey thought more of his Negro helper as a cowboy than he did of Hadley. The story passed down by the other cowhands is that this cowboy froze to death, but the remarkable feature of his passing is that he froze in summertime, July or August.

The Negro cowhand and two other cowboys had been sent out from the ranch to look for some cattle that had drifted before a storm. They had turned the cattle homeward when the Negro complained of feeling cold. The boys made him get down and walk, but he seemed no better for the exercise, so they held him on his horse until they got to the ranch. He was dead when they got there.

He was buried and Dr. Winfrey had a fence built about the grave and planted a willow at the head of it. For years this was the only marked grave in the county. Though the location of the grave is unknown today, one still hears it refered to as "Dead Negro Draw."[75]

For their ranch, the Winfreys decided on a spot with a living spring about one and one-half miles west of the present site

---

[73] Jack Potter. letter to Rose White.1945.

[74] Lone Jack Historical Society. Lone Jack, Missouri.

[75] Rose White. "The H-Bar Ranch." Speech.

of Portales and there they established the H-Bar Ranch. Dr. Winfrey did not settle for the usual dugout or simple sod house as was customary for the rough and tough cowmen from Texas.

According to Cooley Urton, "They filed on four claims, and built a four-room house where the four came together. Each had a room on his own claim: Dr. Winfrey, Hadley, the sister, Mrs. Easley, and the fourth one must have been the negro that afterward froze to death in July. I remember him well."

There was a fireplace in each room, and a hand pump was installed in the kitchen to bring up fresh water from the well. Barns, store houses and corrals were erected, also of adobe.

The Winfreys brought cottonwood switches from Ft. Sumner and when the first ones died, they dug post holes to water and set the trees in these holes. For many years these were the only trees in the whole valley. Winfrey also differed from the usual cowman by planting a garden and peach trees.

Their brand, "H with a Bar" under it, was taken from Hadley's initials, and at first was "H Bar W," but later the "W" was dropped. Sometimes the top section of the "H" was extended so that it reached across the back of the steer, thus the brand was visible on both sides of the animal. The "bar" was always under the "H."[76]

The Winfreys' sister, Mary Josie Easley, by then a widow with three little daughters, Leta, Roma, and Winnie, and a son Joseph, also came to live at the H-Bar. The Winfreys' elderly mother and father often came from Missouri to spend the summer at the ranch. In 1890 Mary received a patent on a parcel of land at the home site and was probably the first duly registered land owner in the Portales Valley.

In 1886 Dr. Hadley Winfrey was called to officiate at the post mortem exam of Gabe Henson after he was shot and killed by Doak Good. In requesting payment from the Lincoln County Commission, he wrote, "At that hot date, August 26, '86, our nearest officer was at Roswell nearly 100 miles away, thus it was quite impracticable to have his additional services, however desirable it might have been."

---

[76] Jack Potter. letter to Rose White.December 7, 1940.

He concluded, "But viewing all the facts in the case, Gentelemen, I hope you'll treat me as kindly as other members of the profession under similar circumstances; tackling an unpleasant (either in odor or otherwise) duty."

He listed his address as "Winfrey Bros. ranch, Staked Plains, N.M., P.O. Fort Sumner, N.M."[77]

The Winfreys tried ranching for several years, but finally decided it was not for them. In 1897 they sold out to Jim Newman and his brother-in-law, Tom Trammell, and returned to Missouri. As far as is known, they never returned to New Mexico.[78]

Picnic at the H-Bar Ranch after 1900. Burns collection.

---

[77]Dr. Hadley Winfrey. letter to Lincoln Co. Commissioners. July 1887. Lincoln County Historical Records.

[78] Rose White. "Times Were Hard." *Portales Daily News*. October 1, 1950.

Dr. Caleb Winfrey. hero of Lone Jack Hill. Collection of
Wilson's Creek National Battlefield. Image courtesy
of the National Park Service.

Jim "Lane" Cook. Courtesy of *The Shamrock*. Spring.1964.

Chapter 16
Jim Cook, Raconteur

One of the most fascinating characters associated with the early history of Roosevelt and Curry Counties was cowman, lawman, gunfighter, and raconteur, James "Jim" Cook.

Dr. Caleb Winfrey and his brother Hadley of Cass County, Missouri, had established the H-Bar Ranch near Portales in 1885. With them came their widowed sister, Mary Josie Easley and her daughters, Leta, Roma, and Winnie, and son Joseph. Mary's husband, Joseph Easley had died in 1883.[79]

The giant XIT Ranch of Texas owned the land just across the New Mexico border. The XIT was divided into seven divisions with a foreman in each division who answered to a general manager.

James "Jim" Cook, a reputed gunman, was hired as foreman of the Escarbada Division with its headquarters close to the little village of La Plata, near where the present town of Hereford is located.

Jim Cook was born in Arkansas, but came to Texas with his family at the end of the Civil War. When he was orphaned at a young age he went to live with an uncle who was a ranchman. For many years he traveled with different herds and on one drive was nicknamed "Jim Lane," or "Kid Boss" by his companions for his arrogant manner.

The huge XIT had many rustlers to contend with, and according to historian J. Evetts Haley, "Jim Cook, wearing his two six-shooters and his ill-boding reputation with equal grace, rode in to do battle with the cow thieves to the west. Aggressive

---

[79] Cass Co. Historical Society. Cass Co. Missouri.

and overbearing, it is said he was eternally at odds with the riders across the line [in New Mexico]."[80]

Jack Potter, who was trail boss for the New England Cattle Company with headquarters in Ft. Sumner, had frequent encounters with Cook and confirms the irascibility of the range foreman. Potter reported that, "Once he wouldn't let me go through the XIT pasture when I was taking a trail herd to Amarillo and I went through at night, twenty-eight miles, a real hardship on the cattle."[81]

The village of La Plata was right on the stage route from Portales Springs to Amarillo and on north to Kansas. Young Leta Easley somehow became acquainted with Jim Cook, presumably as she traveled back and forth to Kansas City from the H-Bar Ranch. Or perhaps Cook visited the H-Bar Ranch on his excursions into New Mexico in pursuit of rustlers of the XIT cattle.

Cook became smitten with the young Miss Easley and in order to avoid having to ride in from ranch headquarters to the neighboring village of La Plata to receive her letters; he finagled to get the Escarbada location designated as a U. S. Post Office. Thus, says Haley, "the young lady's letters would be delivered slap-dab at the ranch house door."

Cook and sixteen-year-old Leta were soon married. They became the parents of two children who were born at the H-Bar Ranch where her uncles, the Drs. Winfrey, could care for her. These two children, Theodore born in 1891 and Minnie born in 1893, were probably the first babies born in what is now Roosevelt County.[82]

When Deaf Smith County, Texas, was formed in 1890, La Plata became the County Seat, and Cook left the XIT to become its first sheriff. But a year later he was kicked out for the

---

[80] J. Evetts Haley. "Jim Cook on the Frontiers of Fantasy." *The Shamrock.* Spring.1964.p. 5.

[81] Jack Potter. letter to Rose White. October 3, 1949.

[82] Family Group Record. Nita Strewart Haley Memorial Library. Midland.Texas.

unnecessary killing of a cowboy. He bragged that since La Plata had no cemetery, he had to kill someone to start one. He was eventually acquitted of the murder.

Cook and his wife Leta and their children wandered from one location to another for several years. In 1908 they were in Albuquerque, New Mexico, when as Cook told Haley, "my poor wife fell by the wayside." What actually happened was that son Theodore came down with a case of appendicitis and Cook departed with daughter Minnie, leaving his son and wife in Albuquerque, never seeing them again.[83]

For many years Cook engaged in various enterprises from prospecting to trail guiding as he and daughter Minnie wandered the U.S. and Canada. He wrote several books and was always ready to entertain anyone who would listen to his tales of adventure.

With the help of Dr. T. M. Pearce of the University of New Mexico, Cook wrote a book, calling himself "Lane of the Llano."[84] In this book, he describes a wild life; being captured by the Comanches as a youth; marrying White Swan, an Indian princess; watching her die from a rattlesnake bite; scouting with Ranald S. McKenzie and Quanah Parker; and being involved with John Chisum and Billy the Kid. He describes many exciting adventures on the trail and on buffalo hunts that defy credibility.

Southwestern author J. Evetts Haley says that, "An accurate biography of Cook could never be written as long as the man failed to distinguish between truth and fiction."

However, the book is a fascinating and accurate description of life on the trail and on the Llano Estacado before the coming of civilization.

---

[83] Theodore Cook. letter to Alice L. Blakemore. December 29, 1976. Haley Memorial Library.

[84] Jim Cook and Dr. T. M. Pearce. *Lane of the Llano*. (Boston: Little, Brown, & Co. 1936.)

Ora White Wood and R. L. "Bob" Wood. Burns Collection.

Chapter 17
Ora and Bob Wood at the H-Bar

When the Winfreys sold the H-Bar Ranch to Jim Newman and Tom Trammell in 1897, Newman asked his cousin, R. L. "Bob" Wood, to take over the ranch as foreman. Bob had come with Newman to the DZ Ranch in 1882 and had worked there as a cowhand ever since.

Bob asked a "widder woman," my grandmother Ora White of Sweetwater, Texas, to be his wife. She accepted and soon she and her two sons, six-year-old R. E., "Eddie," and four-year-old Willis, "Bill," began packing their things for the long trip to the plains of Eastern New Mexico.

The trip from Sweetwater to the New Mexico ranch was made in the early spring, as soon as the grass was good enough to give the horses food on the way.

"It was a hard trip," Mrs. Wood recalled. "We were on the trail eleven days. One of the horses got a lame shoulder, and that is why it took us so long. We followed the Old Fort Sumner Trail, camping at water holes at night. We passed many herds of antelope and wild mustangs. And there were so many birds around the water holes that their squawking kept us awake at night.[85]"

Ora and Bob were in for a pleasant surprise when they reached the H-Bar. Most of the homes on the plains in the 1890s were either dugouts or sod shacks, but the H-Bar house was adobe with a solid roof of boards which were brought all the way from Ft. Sumner. The Woods did not have to worry about water leaking through the roof several days after a big rain.

---

[85] Ora Wood. interview by Rose White. 1932..

The house boasted four rooms, a kitchen, a bunk room for the cowhands, a bedroom, and a living room that could double for another bedroom. There was a fireplace in each of the four rooms. There was large iron stove to cook on and a pump brought fresh water right into the kitchen from a well beneath the house.

Connected to the house were three rooms for groceries, meat, and harness. Across a path were a chicken house, store rooms for grain and saddles, and a blacksmith shop. These sheds opened onto an adobe corral. Behind the corral were two windmills which emptied into a large stock tank.

Another surprise was a garden behind the house and a peach orchard. Shading the ranch house were large, leafy cottonwood trees which had been brought from Ft. Sumner by Dr. Winfrey; the only trees on an otherwise treeless plain.

However all these conveniences did not make for an easy life for a woman in 1890s. Ora's days were filled with household tasks: cooking, washing, ironing, sewing, and mending. Outdoor jobs included tending to the chickens, pigs, and the garden; tasks considered beneath the dignity of the cowboys. Then there was jerky to make, fruit to preserve, soap to make, and the never-ending chore of gathering cowchips for fuel. There was no wood to be had, but mesquite roots were often dug to give a longer lasting blaze.

Besides Ora's family, there were four or five cowboys to cook for, to say nothing of passing ranchers who ate and slept at any nearby place as a matter of course. "Many times I had gotten up in the night and cooked a meal for people I didn't even know," said Mrs. Wood.

There was never any pay offered for these accommodations nor would it have been accepted if it had. The payment took the form of news and gossip, which was better than money to lonely people on the plains. "However," said Ora, "I never cooked for the cowboys at the roundup. Me and the boys went out and ate at the chuckwagon with the cowhands."

As soon as there were neighbors, Mrs. Wood rode to visit them on horseback. Mrs. Mattie Lang, one of the first settlers, has said, "Mrs. Bob Wood was the first to come to see me. She came horseback, riding sidesaddle, on a gray horse. She wore a sunbonnet, and I can still imagine I see her, coming in a high lope across the prairie."

Life on the plains in the 1890s was equally hard on the men as it was on the women.

As foreman of the H-Bar Ranch, Bob Wood was responsible for the health and safety of twenty-five hundred cattle which roamed at will over two-hundred square miles of prairie. The ranch did not own all the land it claimed, only a section where the house stood and forty acres around each windmill, which was held by "script." However the area claimed was strictly respected by neighboring ranches.

The H-Bar Ranch boasted seven windmills on an area that extended in the north to where the railroad tracks now run west to Clovis, the south line about where Delphos now is, the east line toward the Clovis highway, and the west line near Bethel.

At this time there were less than ten houses in all the northern half of the county, and the whole area was claimed by five big ranches: the H-Bar, the DZ at Salt Lake, the Pig Pen at the Tules north of Floyd, the Littlefield LFD west of Elida, and the T-71 near Kenna. In addition there were a few smaller places, such as the Sid Boykin place, the Carter homestead at Tierra Blanca, and the Doak Good spread at Portales Springs.

There was plenty of work for the men to do on the H-Bar. The windmills had to be checked and repaired regularly, for the cattle had to have water at all times. In dry weather there were fire guards to be dug and grass fires to be fought. There were cows to be counted and doctored, and calves to look out for.

As there were no doctors near, the ranchers had to depend on their own simple remedies to take care of sickness and accidents. Also, they had to be resourceful in mending harness or tools, and in half-soling shoes.

There were no fences except for an occasional drift fence put up to keep the cattle from drifting off the range. It was against the law to erect fences, and any barbed wire was quickly taken down if a range inspector was rumored to be in the vicinity. The cattle stayed on their own range pretty well in good weather, but when a storm came, they would start walking, with their backs to a cold wind and snow.

If they were not turned back, they would keep walking until the storm abated, or until they reached the protection of the sandhills around Monahans and Ft. Stockton, Texas.

It was the duty of the cowboys to get out and try to turn the cattle back to their own range. Often the men would stay out all night and all day if the storm was bad. If they could succeed in turning them, the cattle would come on back to water, but if they did not succeed, the cattle were claimed at the spring roundup and brought home.

Thus the purpose of the roundup, conducted every spring and fall, was to sort out the animals of each ranch, brand the new calves, and cut out steers for shipping to market.

The life of the pioneer family was not made any easier by the fact that supplies were brought in only twice a year by trail wagons from Colorado City, Texas.

Dunn's store was the chief general merhandise center for all of west Texas and eastern New Mexico. From there trail wagons drawn by mules or oxen were kept constantly on the roads carrying supplies to the out-lying ranches. Not only food and clothing, but tools, repair parts for harness, wagons, windmills, and lumber for farm buildings, were hauled over the long miles to far-away ranches.

The trips of these slow-moving wagons took several months. Often eight or ten wagons would travel together for mutual help and companionship. Payment for the goods bought was made only once a year after the steers had been sold in the fall.

The foodstuffs hauled in included the following items and very little else: flour in wooden barrels, wooden boxes of dried fruit, kegs of molasses, navy beans in hundred pound sacks, and Arbuckles coffee in one-pound packages, one hundred to the case. Bob Wood often joked that he had won his wife Ora as a premium by saving up the coupons from Arbuckles Coffee.

Of course such things as sugar, salt, soda, tobacco, and matches were also brought by the wagons. Soap was not purchased since it could be made at the ranch. There were no canned vegetables or fruits; nothing fancy such as pickles or ketchup.

In the fall came wagon-loads of grain for the saddle horses. The cattle were never fed, winter or summer, but the saddle horses were given grain all through the cold months. All supplies were stored in adobe rooms adjoining the main house. Mail came from Las Vegas and court was held in Roswell.

The cowboys ate the same thing three times a day, breakfast, dinner, and supper: sourdough biscuits, navy beans, bacon or beef, and coffee. There was usually molasses and sometimes dried fruit. In a country full of cows, there was never milk, cream or butter, because of the cowboys' reluctance to milk the cows.

Beef was always butchered when needed, if the cattle were fat enough. The cowboys ate beef three times a day, roasted or fried or stewed. A rule of the plains helped to keep everybody supplied with meat. This was, that if you didn't have a beef that was fat, it was perfectly legal to kill one belonging to a neighbor.

Of course he could kill one of yours in return, a practice called "swapping beef." Jack Potter once said, in talking of this custom: "It's strange, but the other feller's beef always seemed to be fatter than ours."[86]

Jerky, the thin slices of sun-dried beef that served to fill up the men when the fresh beef was not available, was a necessary item. Pounded up fine, it was made into stew, but it was also eaten raw. Another dish, copied from the Indians, was to mix the pounded jerky with dried fruit for "pemmican." If a man planned to be away from the ranch for several days, he would put a quantity of jerky in his saddle bag, and often this would be his only food until he returned.

In the 1890s grass fires were a constant hazard, just as they are today. However, without the modern equipment and fire fighting methods, a blaze would sweep undiminished for days across miles of open prairie, until it burned itself out or was doused by a rain.

---

[86] Jack Potter. interview by Rose White. September 1949.

After the grass was dry in the fall, every man for miles around would be on the alert and would pitch in to fight the fires, day and night if necessary.

To help prevent this danger, the ranchers would make fireguards: two plowed furrows about twenty feet apart, with the grass burned off between. Each fall it was necessary to renew these guards. It was hard, dirty work, and the women folks were left at home.

Mrs. Ora Wood told the following story of an incident when she and Bob were living at the H-Bar Ranch.

"One fine, sunny November day, Mrs. Nannie Boykin had come to stay with me while the men were out in Black Water Draw burning fireguards. When one of the men came back to the house for more chuck, we decided to go back with him for a little outing.

"We put the children and some food in the buckboard, hitched the horses up and climbed in ourselves. Then we drove over to where the men were working.

"When Bob saw us, he came over to the wagon, and I never saw him so mad. 'You will have to go back home, and right this minute, too. This ain't no place for women and a passel of kids.'"

Mrs. Wood said they went back home, highly incensed at the men folks for ruining their picnic with their unreasonableness. She and the children went to bed with the weather still warm, but awoke to find a blizzard raging outside. Snow lay in drifts everywhere.

The men straggled in a day later. They had had to walk home since their horses and mules had all stampeded. They were worn out, and their feet were blistered from the long walk in the snow.

"So you see, Pa was right after all," said Mrs. Wood. "You never knew about the weather on the plains. It could change overnight."

In the spring when the grass was good, the big spring roundup would begin. Starting below Roswell and working north from ranch to ranch, the cattle were gathered, branded and castrated, and started back to their home ranches. Most of the fights started over ownership of unbranded calves without a mother cow. The rule everywhere agreed upon was that such a calf belonged to the man on whose range it was found. Usually ten or twelve men were hired for the roundup in contrast to the six or seven kept for summer work. At least four horses per man were used at each roundup.

In the late summer a second roundup gathered all the straying cattle. The steers were then driven to market, at first to Dodge City or Hayes City, Kansas. Later, as the railroads came west, they were taken for shorter distances, until finally they were driven only to Amarillo and then to Portales when the railroad reached there.

"After we had been at the H-Bar four years," Mrs. Wood recalled, "we leased the school section north of town and later managed to trade for the place west of it. The man that owned the place was glad to trade the 160 acres for a balky horse. We told him the horse was balky, but he was so anxious to leave that he traded anyway."

Mrs. Wood, at age seventy-six, looked back on those days with a smile. "Sure we had hard times; harder than modern people will ever know. But we had good times, too. When the railroad came in 1898, we soon had neighbors pretty close, and so we weren't so lonely. Then there were picnics and parties, and we all got together and had a good time.

"The first Fourth of July picnic was held in the new lumber yard on the east side of the new little town. There were no fireworks, but there was a race of saddle ponies down Main Street, and a speech by a politician from Texas known as 'Sockless Jerry.' The women of the town baked pies, and the men provided coffee, pickles, meat, and bread. This was in 1899.

"Every summer, in those early days, we would all go to the sandhills to gather wild plums. There were a great many plum bushes in those days, and the plums were not stunted as they are now. We could have gathered twenty-five wagon loads of them if we had wanted to, but we only took what we could use. Everyone would go to gather plums, as these were the only fruit in the valley; and we made a holiday of the trip, taking our lunch, and having a regular picnic of it."

The railroad reached the ranch land in 1898 brought an end to the long cattle drives to the northern railheads. With the railroad, also came the homesteaders, derisively called "nesters" by the cattlemen. As Buster DeGraftenreid said, "What a change there was in every way. The nesters was coming and HELL broke loose when the railroad got from Texico to Belen.[87]

Bob and Ora Wood and sons Eddie and Bill White at the H-Bar Ranch. 1898.

---

[87] Buster DeGraftenreid. letter to Rose White. January 24, 1940.

Chapter 18
Young Boys on the Prairie

The prairie in the early days was a wonderful place for small boys. The grown-ups were busy with their chores and didn't have a lot of time to spend worrying about the young'uns. Consequently little boys could spend their time exploring, chasing rabbits, following the cowboys, and very often getting into mischief.

When my father Eddie White and his brother Bill came with their mother Ora to the H-Bar Ranch in 1897, they were six and four years old respectively, just old enough to be curious about everything.

Strangers often came by the ranch, and one morning when all the adults were gone, a man rode up who was pretty drunk. He said he wanted to borrow a shotgun and shoot some of the ducks that were on the tank.

Eddie told the story, "Neither Pa nor Ma were at home, but we said me and Bill would lend him a gun. We got down the shotgun, and said we would be glad to load it for him. Well, we really did load it: tamped down the powder, poured in the shot, and then tamped it down hard with wet newspaper. That way, it will really kick. The man went reeling off to the tank, and Bill and I followed, about to bust with trying not to laugh.

"Well, when he fired the darn gun, it knocked him flat, so that he fell right under his horse. He picked himself up, climbed on the horse, and rode away, cussing a blue streak. He just left the gun laying on the ground where it fell. Bill and I laughed over that for weeks, but we never told it to Ma and Pa till after we were grown."[88]

---

[88] Eddie White. interview by Rose White.1932.

Ora always told the children not to dare to try any bronco riding when they were little fellows. Eddie remembered, "When we was ten or eleven, she was still saying, 'Don't you dare to try to ride them broncs. If one was to throw you, you might get killed.' Finally, when she was saying this one day, she turned to a cowboy who was setting at the table drinking coffee, and says, 'What are you grinning for?'

"'Why,' says he, 'Them boys has been riding broncs over in the sand hills for more'n three years. They ride a lot better than some of us do.' We had been throwed heaps of times, but the sand was softer than the hard ground, and it never hurt us much."

Eddie recalled one time when the boys nearly caused trouble with the neighbors. "Ma and Pa were gone to court in Roswell once when about six or seven colts came wandering up to the H-Bar Headquarters, and Bill and I got them into the adobe corral.

"We snubbed them down and clipped all the long hair off their manes and tails and stuffed it in a tow sack and hid it back of some feed in the barn. Then we turned them loose. The next morning, a bunch of nesters came up, mad as hell. They all had guns, and they came to see what the H-Bar men meant by ruining their colts. Somebody was going to get hurt, sure, it looked like.

"Pa says, 'Why, we don't know nothing about it. We've all been to Roswell to court; got home late last night. There wasn't nobody here but these little boys.'

"The men all went grumbling off, and we didn't get punished. Nobody thought we were big enough to handle those colts. One of the cowboys helped us make a rope out of the hair and never did tell on us."

Eddie loved to follow his stepfather Bob Wood and the other cowhands as they roped and rode and tended to the cattle. The cowboys were good-natured and tolerated the youngster with a lot of patience. Eddie has said, "Pa let me go out with him and the cowboys when they went out to round up the cattle. I would help the cook, gather up cowchips for the fire, go get the horses and do whatever odd jobs they could find for me.

"At night I slept in the cooney, or *cuña* in Spanish. The cooney, also called the 'possum belly,' was a bull hide stretched under the chuckwagon to carry the pots and pans and cowchips for the fire, but it made a good bed for me up off the ground and out of the way of rattlesnakes.

"Once, when I was seven or eight years old, Pa got me up early and told me to go and drive in the horses so the men could rope out their mounts. We were working from the wagon at the time. I got me a cup half full of whiskey and started out.

"It was just getting light, and, as I went over a little hill, the sun came up. Everything looked pretty and fresh, and a little cool breeze was blowing. I found the horses right away, and started back. They weren't hard to drive.

"All of a sudden, the day, which had been so bright and sunny, began to get dark. I looked up, and there wasn't a cloud in the sky. It got darker and darker, till finally it was nearly as dark as night, and some stars began to shine. I really was scared, and I ran the last part of the way to the wagon.

"When I got there, I found that the cowboys, and even Pa, were frightened, too. 'Hit's the end of the world,' said Pa. 'We'd better get to prayin'.' About then the light began to come back, and in a little while, it was a fine sunny day. That was a total eclipse of the sun. I never will forget how scared I was."

Roundup on the Bar-V. Cooley Urton Collection. Courtesy
The New Mexico Stockman. 1949.

Chapter 19
The Early Day Cowboy

The cowboy of the Llano Estacado was a unique individual who came into being in the early days, originating in Texas and ranging out over the West, wherever cattle were raised.

The cattle industry started in Texas after the Civil War. Cattle had been pretty much allowed to run free while men were off fighting in the war, and many of them roamed and reproduced in the brush country without interference of man. After the war, enterprising individuals, seeing the need for beef in the north, began to round up these longhorn cattle and drive them to markets in Kansas and other northern markets.[89]

This whole Llano Estacado was a rolling plain with high grass and little water. There was one trail leading across the north end of the county by way of the little chain of surface lakes from Texas to Fort Sumner. Very few people traveled this road; most of the freighters and cattlemen would rather go a longer route and miss this lonely stretch with no houses for two hundred miles.

Before the ranchers came, this vast grassy plain was occupied only by the buffalo, the antelope, and the lobo wolf. Occasionally Indians and other hunters would cross the plains following the herds of antelope and buffalo.

In an interview in 1949, Jack Potter said, "Many hunters from the Pecos settlements eighty miles away went to Portales Springs to kill buffalo and antelope for their winter's supply of meat, and often such men as old Ramon Silva and the Celedon and Trujillos brothers went there to hunt mustangs. Old Vicente Otero, who died at Fort Sumner a few years ago at the age of 105, told me fifty years ago that he and a man named Silva hunted for

---

[89] J. Frank Dobie, *The Longhorns*, (Boston: Little, Brown, & Co. 1941.)

buffalo and antelope and caught mustangs at Portales Spring when he was a boy."[90]

There had been cowboys called *vaqueros* in Mexico for many years and many of the terms used by the American cowboy had their origin in the Spanish language. For instance: there is lasso, *lazo*, lariat, *la reata*, bar-b-que, *barbacoa*, stampede, *estampeda]*, chaps, *chaparreras*, mustang, *mesteño*, jerky, *chaqui*, hoosegow, *juzgado, rodeo, bronco, remuda*, and *corral*.

The man who wished to be a cowboy had to be tough. He had to be able to withstand long days in the saddle in all kinds of weather. He had to go for long periods of time away from civilization with meager food and little shelter. He had to deal with balky cows, wild animals, outlaws, stampedes, wind, rain, and snow with very little pay and no security. The ranches were few and far between and the work was hard and monotonous.

Jack Potter said of the early day cowboy, "They were real men. Just think of us cowboys working sixteen hours per day, enduring those sand storms and drinking that Pecos river water that was strong enough to kill seven hundred Navajo Indians."

During the year, ranch work consisted mainly of caring for the horses and keeping the windmills repaired. The cattle grazed over a large unfenced area and windmills were situated at strategic places, as there was no surface water. Half-dugouts were used as line camps on the far-flung reaches of the ranch for men caught out on the llano overnight.

Winter work was the hardest. According to E. L. Stephens, the nighttime was long and lonesome. "The wind would blow and wolves would howl and skunks would come on the porch and fight. And the big blue rats. We called them pack rats for they would carry everthing loose. We had to keep everything pulled from the table we set on, if we didn't the rats would get on the table and carry everyhthing off the table."[91]

Sometimes only a few men would remain at the ranch house and they would be responsible for tending to the windmills and keeping the cattle from drifting in a storm. As long

---

[90] Jack Potter. interview by Rose White.1949.

[91] E. L. Stephens. *"Recollections of a Young Cowboy."* Unpublished manuscript.

as the cattle could keep walking, they would not freeze, and would often drift as far as the sandhills near Monahans, Texas, before stopping. If the cattle were stopped by a fence, those following would pile up until they could climb over the frozen bodies of their companions.

Dan McFatter said, "In winter, when the cattle drifted south ahead of storm, we would usually get out as soon as we could and try to turn them. Then they would usually come on back to their own pasture. We usually stayed out two nights; took water, food, and a tent to sleep in. This was called a 'floating outfit.'"[92]

It was easy to get bored out on the plains. Col. Potter recalled one incident when the cowboys tried to tame a wolf cub:

"There were lots of wolves in the early days. The Tulies was the worst place. At the last, the wolves like to et us up. Near the Tulies one time we came on a place that was full of wolf dens. We killed one bunch. The next was a little bigger. John Hull said, 'I'll take one home for a pet.'

"He took it home seven miles on his horse and tied it up. The wolf wouldn't eat or drink. The mother sat on a hill near camp and barked all night. Next day the pup wouldn't eat again. Lon Reed said, 'I'll stake him out and let him nurse his mother.' So he staked him out a little piece from camp. In ten minutes the mother had cut the rope and taken the pup away. How she followed our trail all that seven miles I don't know."

The food was monotonous. Supplies were brought from Colorado City, Texas, twice a year, and the cook had to make do with whatever was on hand. The food at the ranch or on the trail consisted of coffee, bacon, navy beans, sourdough biscuits, sometimes dried fruit or molasses, and beef three times a day, fried, roasted, or stewed.

Potter said, "We didn't eat bacon much. We used bacon on branding irons and to start the fire when wood was wet. We ate beef mostly. When on the roundup, we'd kill a beef every two days. A beef from one outfit, then the other and divide. The rule

---

[92] Dan McFatter. interview by Rose White. 1939.

was to kill a fat beef, whatever brand it had. We called it 'swapping beef.' Mostly we killed the other fellows'. It was surprising how often his beef was fatter than ours."

Large amounts of beef were dried and made into jerky. No man would start out on a journey without a supply of jerky in his saddlebags, and that might be his only food for days.

Cowboy Dan McFatter said, "At the DZ Ranch, Jim Newman always fed good. In the fall he'd say, 'Now, boys, don't forget you'll need some jerky this winter. Be sure and make you enough to last you.' We'd butcher a beef, and slice it up nice and thin, then hang it on lines. We'd dry it till it was hard as a board. Then we'd put it in towsacks and stack it away for winter."

A man's horses were essential to his being able to perform his work. According to Potter, "A remuda was the horses for a change of mounts. Each man had about six for the trail, ten or twelve for roundup. We would change horses four times a day. We had one that was good at cutting out cows. Tom Love could rope fifteen or twenty horses in just a little while."

Cooley Urton of the Bar-V Ranch has said, "Cattle were never counted on the range. When an owner turned a herd loose, he knew how many there were at that time. He kept a record of the increase branded, those sold, and estimated the loss by rustlers and death. This was all he knew until he gathered and disposed of them."[93]

Thus, the roundup was held twice a year to sort out the cattle, brand the increase, and return them to their home range. The roundup started at the southernmost range to which the cattle had drifted and included all the neighboring ranches. They worked together with a general boss in charge. This boss was the one on whose land the roundup had reached that day and passed to the boss of each range as the roundup progressed.

Urton described the roundup, "When work once started, it was an all day and night job. The day started at daybreak with breakfast and lasted till sundown. The night work commenced then. Each man on the crew had to take his share of the night guard. The guard periods varied in length according to the

---

[93] Cooley Urton."Roundup on the Pecos," *New Mexico Stockman,* June 1949.

number of men in the crew. There were guards for the cattle and others for the horses.

"The cattle bedded down and were quiet all night, unless there was a storm or stampede. In this case, the guard was often one-half night, or even all night. The horse guards had to be on the move all night as horses graze at night with the exception of about two hours. From two to four a.m. most of them sleep.

"The mavericks and dogies in each indiviual roundup were considered the property of the owner of the range on which it was found. This often caused disputes on account of overlapping claims. This was generally settled in a fair and gentlemanly manner, though the .45 Colt was sometimes the deciding factor.

"The cow and calf cut was held near the branding fire by part of the crew. Another part was set aside in pairs to flank and hold the calves as they were dragged to the fire. The roper called the brand to be placed on the differnt calves as he dragged them to the fire. The flankers told the man with the hot iron the brand to place on the calf they were holding.

"The man with the hot iron stood back of the animal. He had to place the brand so it would read right when the animal was on foot. This was quite a knack so none but the experienced were qualified for this job. A man versed in the various ear marks did the earmarking and castrating. Vaccinating was unheard of and there was no dehorning as horns were considered a means of defense."

The early day cowboy did not wear the typical outfit of the movie cowboy, you may be sure. Leather chaps were sometimes worn in the winter, for warmth, but not in the summer. There was no need of them on the open plains where there was little brush. Wide hats were necessary to keep off the sun and rain, as was a neckerchief to protect the face from the clouds of dust. Ordinary shirts were common; and very heavy, brown and white checked trousers, known as "California pants" were the usual. Boots and spurs were worn when riding, but they were for service, not for show. A slicker was necessary for wet weather, and an overcoat for winter.

Each cowboy had a bed roll consisting of plenty of heavy blankets and "sugans," or quilts, a tarpaulin, and some times a Navajo blanket or two. Most of the cowboys owned six-shooters, but kept them in their bed rolls, and only used them sparingly. Every cowboy owned a suit of store clothes, to dress up in when he went to town, and a pair of good shoes or boots to go with it.

On Saturday afternoons when not on a round-up, the young cowpunchers would sometimes ride to Fort Sumner to attend the regular Saturday night dances. It was a sixty or seventy-five mile ride, but they thought nothing of using most of their leisure for the trip back and forth, in order to have the pleasure of dancing a few hours with the pretty Mexican girls of old Fort Sumner. Of course these young ladies were accompanied by their mothers in their black dresses and mantillas, who sat nearby and kept a stern eye out for any inappropriate behavior. The trip back home was made on Sunday. Occasionally the boys would ride as far as Roswell to dance, when they could be spared for the long trip back and forth.

Of course, the cowpunchers of the Eighties and Nineties were no angels. When they were paid off, thirty dollars and board was the usual wage, they went to town and celebrated; got drunk, played poker, sometimes lost every dime they had earned. In a country where there was scarcity of peace officers, the wonder is that the fights and killings were not more numerous.

On the whole the men were too busy to get into much mischief. They did not go to church, but they had a very real and true religion; its motto was, "Help your friend when he needs you." These pioneer cowboys were rough, uneducated, hard-working, but they were gentlemen at heart, as was proved by their kindness and loyalty to each other.[94]

Cooley Urton has said of the old-time cattlemen: "As a rule I knew them as a very high type men. I have often heard said of many of them that their word was just as good as a bond, and this was my observation as a rule. Any that did not live up to expectation soon moved on."

---

[94] White, Rose. "The Valley in 1880." *Portales News-Tribune.*1940,

Billy Dixon, survivor of the Adobe Walls fight said, "That was the way of the West in those times--every tub had to stand on its own bottom every minute of the day. It was the code that every able-bodied man had to live by. If, however, a man should fall sick or be in bad luck or crippled, the boys stuck to him until he was able to take care of himself."[95]

Buster DeGraftenreid had this to say, "No, there wasn't many fights. Now and then there would be a misunderstanding between some ranch and their men, and someone would get killed. Right now there is and always was a right and a wrong way. The wrong way never did pay and never will. Get right and stay right. Make the other fellow let you alone. If you are right, he will, all right."[96]

Jack Potter was emphatic in his feelings: "The cowboy was never classed as a common laborer. He was welcomed to society anywhere, and the whole U.S. tries to imitate a cowboy in dress. It gives the Big Ones such as Teddy Roosevelt a thrill to wear a Ten-Gallon Stetson and look like a cowboy."[97]

One cannot help feeling that some of their straight dealings and clean living has been instilled into their descendants, the present inhabitants of Eastern New Mexico; and that a friendliness and a comradeship still remains as a precious heritage from these early settlers, the ranchers and cowboys of the Llano Estacado.

---

[95] Olive Dixon. *Life of Billy Dixon*. (Austin: State House Press. 1987) p. 189.

[96] Buster DeGraftenreid .letter to Rose White.January 4, 1940..

[97] Potter. letter to Rose White. February 13, 1950.

Cowboys and Chuck Wagon. Courtesy of ENMU Golden Library
Special Collections.

Chapter 20
Cowboy Cooks

The cook was one of the most important workers on the ranches of the High Plains. In a country where the cowboys worked from pre-dawn to dark in all kinds of weather, it was vital to have hot, nourishing food ready for them. During the year, ranch work consisted mainly of caring for the horses and keeping the windmills repaired. The cattle grazed over a large unfenced area and windmills were situated at strategic places, as there was very little surface water. The men were out long hours, checking windmills, looking for stray cattle, and at times, fighting grass fires.

For most of the year the cook was headquartered at the ranch house with a large iron stove to cook on. His main problem was getting enough cowchips and mesquite roots to keep a hot fire going. The cowhands helped with this task, but if they were busy, the job fell to the cook. A good supply of fuel had to be maintained in a storage building, for in wet or snowy weather, none could be gathered from the prairie.

Supplies were brought in twice a year in trail wagons from Colorado City, Texas. They consisted mainly of coffee, flour, navy beans, slabs of bacon, and occasionally, boxes of dried fruit or barrels of molasses. Naturally beef was the main staple of the diet.

At the round-up or on a trail drive, the cook had to prepare his meals over a campfire in all kinds of weather and carry all his supplies and pots and pans with him. Charles Goodnight is credited with devising the first chuckwagon with a dropdown door for a table and shelves for supplies. There was a bull-hide, called the cooney or sow-belly, stretched under the wagon for pots and pans. The importance of the chuckwagon was described by J. Evetts Haley in his book, "The XIT Ranch of Texas":

"All of the men lived with the chuck wagon from the breaking of spring until the northers of December. Wherever they spread their bed rolls and stuffed their hats and boots under their heads for pillows, wherever the chuck wagon camped and the cook yelled, 'chuck-away,' 'chuck,' or 'come and get it,' there was home for the cowboys.

"Bolted into the rear end of the wagon was the chuck box. The hinged 'lid' or cover opened from the top and was supported horizontally by a single prop to form a table. Convenient drawers held tin plates, cups, and cutlery. Other drawers and shelves were stored with coffee, tins of sugar, salt, soda, molasses or 'lick,' lard, and other articles of frequent demand. In the bed of the wagon the cook carried a large amount of flour, raisins, sugar, dried fruit, some cases of canned goods, and a reserve supply of 'lick.'"[98]

Rose White published a story in the Western Folklore Record describing one of the mainstays of the cowboy diet, sourdough biscuits:[99]

"Famous in all stories about cowboys and cattle camps are the sourfdough biscuits, the only bread baked on the early day ranches of the plains of Eastern New Mexico and West Texas. Yet many people do not know what a sourdough biscuit is like. The name suggests a heavy, soggy lump with a distinctly sour taste. Nothing could be farther from the truth. Rightly made, the biscuit resembled a light roll, white and fluffy on the inside, with a crisp brown crust. Many a camp cook gained his reputation on the quality of his biscuits, and 'Old Sourdough' was a term of approbation rather than of insult.

"Necessary to the making were flour, salt, sugar, lard, and the 'starter;' which was a sour batter kept in a crock with a rag tied over the top. A large amount of flour was placed in a shallow pan, and a depression was made in the center. Into this hole went

---

[98] J. Evetts Haley, *The XIT Ranch of Texas.* (Norman: University of Olkahoma Press.1936) p. 150.

[99] Rose White, "The Sourdough Biscuit." *Western Folklore.* April, 1956. p. 93.

some batter, salt, sugar, a handful of lard, and enough soda to counteract the acid in the starter. This was all mixed with the hand, the surrounding flour being stirred in with the same motion. No breadboard was needed, and no rolling pin or biscuit cutter. When the dough was of the proper consistency, it was shaped into balls with a tablespoon dipped in hot grease.

"The proper fire was one of hot glowing coals, with little or no flame. The Dutch oven was now hot, and well-greased. The biscuits were rolled around in the grease, and placed close together all over the bottom of the oven. The lid was put on, and a shovel-full of hot coals was placed on top. Now one can see the reason for the rim around the lid. It was to hold the hot coals. Thus, the biscuits were baked from above as well as from below, and the result was a fine, well-baked bread, as delicious as any that can be baked in a modern oven.

"When you ask any of the old cowboy cooks how the 'starter' was started, you are always in for an argument. You see, a crock of starter would stay fresh for years, because new material was added each time to equal the amount taken out, so the batter never got old. Therefore, unless some accident happened to the crock, there was no need to start a new supply. If such an accident did occur, there was no bread for several days, since it took that long for a new mixture to sour. Though the ingredients vary, some would put yeast, while others insist that peach-tree leaves should be used. All agree that flour, water, and sugar are mixed to form a soft batter, and are left to sour in a warm place.

"Woe betide the joker who bothered that sourdough crock! The wrath of all the cowboys, as well as of the cook, would descend upon his unlucky head. Arthur Jones, known as the 'cowboy banker' of Portales, tells the true story of the outlaw who was being hotly pursued by the sheriff and his posse because he was escaping with some stolen twenty-dollar gold pieces. Galloping up to a cowcamp, he looked around for a place to hide the gold.

"He decided on the one place where the sheriff would never dare to look; the one thing that nobody ever interfered with under any circumstances; the crock of sourdough starter. That is where the outlaw hid the gold pieces; he dropped them into the batter where they immediately sank from sight. When the posse arrived, a few minutes later, they searched everywhere, but could not find the gold. The sacredness of that crock was so instilled into them that it never occurred to them that anyone would have the temerity to bother it."[100]

The sourdough biscuit was a sure test of the cooking skill of a new ranch chef. If he could make good biscuits, he could certainly boil a pot of beans, fry steak, or brew a pot of coffee. That was all one had to do to satisfy a crew of hungry men on a ranch in pioneer days in the Old West.

Potter told of a prior type of biscuit, "Before sourdough became steady fare, the early day cooks on these drives did not have to have any experience cooking. Most of them were only asked if they knew how to drive two yoke of steers. My first drives on the trail the cooks made soda bread, sometimes baking powder. Soda bread was bacon grease, water and soda mixed with the flour.

"My first sourdough biscuit eaten were cooked by an old experienced Mexican cook, named Severo Atencio, known as 'Chiquite.' This was at Fort Sumner on the Pecos in 1885. When four Northern companies bought Old Fort Sumner and established headquarters for large herds of cattle, they brought along the bosses and cooks from the Northern locations that were sold. It seems as if the Northern outfits had to teach the Southern ranchers how to take better care of their punchers.[101]"

The cowboys had many stories of camp cooks. Dan McFatter of the DZ Ranch told of the cook hired by the boss, Jim Newman:[102] "Jim found the cook Foster nearly dead of tuberculosis, felt sorry for him, and took him back with him to the DZ Ranch. No one thought of being afraid of germs in those days. Jim made Foster drink fresh blood every day. Foster objected loudly, said he'd rather die; but Newman insisted. Foster got well, and did not forget to be grateful for his boss's kindness.

---

[100] Arthur Jones. interview by Rose White. 1945.

[101] Jack Potter. letters to Rose White. 1940-1950.

[102] Dan McFatter. interview by Rose White. Sept. 1939.

"Let me tell you how Foster cooked a batch of beef one time, that was the best beef I ever et: We was on the trail and we come to a place where there was lots of mesquite wood. It was a bad spell, and we was going to have to keep a fire all night. The boys had been butchering a beef, and Foster asked them for the head. He told them to cut it off as close to the shoulders as they could, so as to leave all of the neck. Well, he wropt it up in gunny sacks, hide and all, dug a hole about two feet deep, and put it in. He said, 'Boys, I'll need a big fire all night.'

"So the boss sent half of us boys, four or five, to get wood. We tied the mesquite wood to a rope fastened to our saddle horns and drawed it in that away. We brought enough to keep a hot fire all night. Foster built his fire right over the hole where he had put the head. The next morning when he raked the fire off, the sacks was not even burned. When he took the sacks off, the hide was a brown crust over the meat.

"He seasoned it up, and I declare, it was the best barbecue I ever saw. We ate off of it all the way to Colorado City. There was ten of us in all; the boss, the cook, and eight men; two and a half hour watches. The cook would heat that meat in a big Dutch oven, and we would eat till we nearly busted. I never tasted such fine meat before or since."

Some cooks became a little cantankerous. According to McFatter, "Once Jim Warren came in late to the chuck wagon and wanted breakfast. The cook was a Dutchman and had a high squeaky voice. He says, 'Breakfast's all out,' pretty cross. Jim says, 'Git me some coffee.' The cook says, 'All gone.' Jim Warren reached for the coffee pot, but the cook kicks it over into the fire before Jim can get it.

"Jim drew his gun and aimed it at the cook. He sure meant to shoot. He said, 'You git me some breakfast.' That cook hurried to the cooney, we called it the sow-belly, under the wagon where he kept some dry kindlin' and chips, and he had a new fire goin' in no time. He made Jim some new coffee and a nice breakfast. After that Jim had no more trouble."

Other cooks went to extraordinary trouble to supply the hungry cowboys with food. McFatter related that once when he was with a herd of cattle going to market:

"It rained for seventeen days, off and on; filled all the lakes; but the trail was so muddy the chuck wagon would bog down every little while. The boys would have to tie their ropes to the saddle horns and the other end to the wagon and he'p it along. There was seventeen days of this rain and mud, and it got mighty tiresome, I can tell you. Then the weather cleared and they thought the bad weather was over.

"But while we was there, it started rainin' again. It had been such a hot, clear day that the orders was: 'Boys, leave your slickers on the chuck wagon.' It rained, rained, rained, and we had no slickers and no time to get 'em. I never was so wet in all my life. By night we had got all the herd across the creek, but then the cook tried to cross with the chuck wagon and right in the middle he got stuck.

"That poor cook worked all night. First he got the mules, then the bedding, then the food. Finally he brought out the wagon bed; took the boards apart and brought it a piece at a time.

"Next morning, when I woke up, there was just the running gear, still stuck in the creek. At sun-up the cook had a five gallon can of coffee steaming on the fire. Breakfast was all ready, too. I says to him, 'How in the world did you manage to git out?' He replies, 'I had to git out. These cowboys had to have their breakfast on time.'"

Such was the dedication of these old-time cooks to the men who depended on hot coffee and warm biscuits when they came in from the dusty, demanding work of herding cattle.

Chapter 21
Cowboy Humor

The life of a cowboy on the Staked Plains was monotonous in the extreme. Lacking, as he did, all means of amusing himself, lacking newspapers and books, lacking for weeks on end, any contact with towns or strangers; he was forced of necessity to fall back on his own resources for his amusement. A man who would think up a good joke was always welcome, and a good storyteller could find an audience around any campfire.

Most of the jokes were of the rough-and-ready variety. Some of them were cruel and some jokes were dangerous to the life of the victim; but this was a society of hardened pioneers, and a "softy" did not last long. "Better find at once if he is able to stand pioneer conditions; if he isn't, he won't stay long out here," seemed to be the way the cowboys reasoned when it came to playing jokes on tenderfeet.

The tenderfeet were usually the victims of the roughest jokes, but a new cowhand could always expect to come in for his share, too. The old hands were not always safe, and even the boss was sometimes "ribbed" unmercifully. Let me tell you some of the stories of cowboy humor, and you can judge for yourself just how much they were enjoyed, not only at the time, but in the retelling for many years thereafter.[103]

Jack Potter reminisced, "One of our greatest pleasures was making up jokes and playing them on tenderfeet. One time when we was coming from Las Vegas, we got to telling the 'greenhorns' in our party about the danger of Indians, and about the frightful massacres that had taken place along this very trail. When we

---

[103] Rose White. "Cowboy Humor." *New Mexico Folklore Record.* Vol.III. 1948-49.

had them good and scared, part of our men slipped away, pretending they wanted to hunt for fresh meat. They slipped ahead and hid behind some big rocks along the trail.

"When we come along, they started shooting, and we yelled, 'Indians!' and started shooting, too. You should have seen those Easterners turn pale. We drove the Indians away, of course, and the tenderfeet had a big thrill out of telling how the party had been attacked, and had barely escaped with their lives. Well, at least till somebody told them that there hadn't been any Indians in that part of New Mexico in ten years.

"One time on the Hondo we had a good joke on a tenderfoot. There was a rough-looking man from the 'Y' Ranch with us named Grizzly Bill. We had him stripped and chained to a wagon-tongue. When the tenderfoot came along, we told him we had caught a wild man that we found living in the mountains.

"We took him to see this horrible creature, and there was Grizzly Bill growling and snarling and chewing on a big chunk of raw meat. As the tenderfoot stood there gaping, Bill broke his chain and started to chase him. The tenderfoot ran for hours, and nearly died of fright. We laughed over that joke for weeks."[104]

Dan McFatter had many stories of pranks played on unsuspecting cowboys, and was himself the subject of several jokes. He related what happened when he first started cowboying, "In May, a big outfit come through Abilene with three herds of cattle, ten thousand head in all. A friend told me they was on their way to Trinidad, Colorado. It was rainin' all the time, and the work was so hard that a lot of the cowhands was quittin'.

"That sounded just like what I wanted, so I went and met the boss, who gave me a job and sent me to camp with orders to the horse wrangler to catch me a horse. I drew my pay for what was coming to me on my old job, and stopped by town where I spent it on a new saddle, boots, spurs, big hat, and slicker, bed roll and, of course, a gun.

"When I got to camp and told the hoss wrangler what his boss had said, he picked me out a hoss. I noticed it was fatter than any of the others, so I said, 'Mister, why is this hoss fatter than any of

---

[104] Jack Potter. interview by Rose White.1949.

those others?' He answered, 'Well, you see, Kid, each cowboy has his own favorite mounts; this is just an extra, and he's fat because he hasn't been working.'

"But he looked kinda funny, and I got suspicious that the hoss was an outlaw. He caught the hoss, and we put my new saddle on him and I climbed on. Well sir! That was the out-pitchin'est hoss I'd ever seen. He pitched and he pitched and he pitched. Finally, I panted out, 'I don't believe I can ride this hoss, mister.'

"'Don''t let the boss hear you say that,' said the hoss wrangler, 'He'll fire you right now.'

"'I don't care if he does,' I says, 'I got a good job haulin' rock waitin' for me in town, and I'm goin' back to it. I'm 'fraid I can't ride him.' I managed to slide off while I was talkin'.

"'Listen,' says the wrangler, 'You do what I tell you and you'll be all right. Don't pull on that hoss's bridle reins. Now you do what I say. Don't pull on the reins.' He told me twicet. 'He'll be all right if you don't pull.'

"Then he put a rolled up blanket on the saddle and I got back on. The outlaw pitched as hard as ever, but he could not get me off. When the cowboys come in at night and turned their hosses loose, one of them asked me if I knew my hoss had killed the last man that tried to ride him.

"When I got a chance, I asked the wrangler if that was so. He says, 'Yes, it's so. The man that was killed, pulled him up and the hoss fell back on him and crushed him. Since then all the boys have been afraid to ride him.'

"It was a cruel way to treat a newcomer, but it was no different from the way I've seen 'em act lots of times. They would not have cared if I had been killed. It would have been a good joke on me."[105]

McFatter continued with another incident, "When I first come to the DZ Ranch, the boys loved to tease me. One cold night we all got to playing cards. Well, it was cold outside, but we had a good fire, and the room was hot as an oven. The boys got to telling how the heat would warm the rattlesnakes that was nesting in the adobe walls. They kept on about the snakes, just as

---

[105] Dan McFatter. interview by Rose White. 1939.

serious as could be. After a while I got tired of playing cards and went to bed.

"Then one of the boys slipped out and took the broom with him. He let the handle get right cold, then slipped back and ran it in under the covers of my bunk and across my bare legs. Of course I thought it was a snake and I let out a yell and kicked the covers nearly to the ceiling, and jumped out of bed like a snake had really bit me.

"But that wasn't the end of the joke. The funniest part to them was the way I hunted that snake. I stayed up most of the night looking for it. The boys just let me hunt; never cracked a smile till they got to joshing me about it the next day."

The boss of the ranch also liked to play jokes said McFatter: "Jim Newman had his own peculiar idea of a joke. Jim Warren was a great friend of mine. Older than most of the cowboys, and crippled up with rheumatism, he was bitter as an east wind. But he was always good to me, and I liked him. Jim Newman had given Warren an easy, gentle horse named Old Glenn, and he kept this animal for his special mount, as he was very stiff.

"Well, one time Jim Newman came to the DZ Ranch bringing with him a spoiled horse; a mean one with a bad reputation. He said, 'Boys, I've brought this new hoss with me. His name is Old Tarpaulin. I'm not going to make any of you take this horse, but I want to use him, and someone has to ride him. Jim Warren, you're the oldest, you'll have to try him.' Jim Warren spoke up quick and says, 'I want Old Glenn.'

"Newman was about to answer that he'd have to ride Old Tarp, when I speak up quick and says, 'I'll take him, Mr. Newman, I'll ride him.' Jim didn't think I could do it; he says, 'You'll have to show me.' Jim Warren went with me to help me saddle up. He says, 'Mac, take every advantage of him you can. He's mean; don't give him a chance.' We fixed a rolled up blanket on the saddle, so he couldn't throw me against the saddle horn.

"I climbed on, and Jim Newman and all the boys crowded out to see the fun. I found out that this hoss had a system; he pitched steady and regular, pitch, pitch, pitch; he kept on and on and on till I thought he'd never stop. I stuck on, tho, till I was plumb give out; but by that time, Old Tarpaulin was, too; and he quit just about the time I thought I couldn't stand any more.

"Jim Warren helped me off, and Jim Newman says, 'Boys, take off your hats to DZ Mac. He's the best rider on the DZ.' They all cheered, but I says, 'There's lots of better riders here, Jim, and you know it. I just rode to keep Jim Warren off of him.'"

The men at the DZ returned the compliment to Newman: "One time Jim Newman arrived at the ranch in his town clothes: store suit, dress shirt, and, of all things, a derby hat! The cowboys pretended they didn't know him. They bowed and scraped, and said, as polite as could be, 'Howdy, Stranger. Won't you stay for dinner? We ain't got much that will appeal to your city appetite, but you are welcome to anything we got.'

"Jim cussed a blue streak, but the men continued to josh him. They kept up the pretense that he was just a tenderfoot, and as such, was the target for practical jokes. They gave him a pair of leather chaps, and they told him he had to ride a mean mule that was almost impossible to conquer.

"Jim could ride any horse on the Plains, but he was not sure he could ride that mule. Nevertheless, he mounted, and though the mule twisted and turned, he could not pitch Jim off. When he rode back to camp, he was dusty and sweaty, and he had lost the derby hat. The men knew him now. 'Why, howdy, Jim,' they said, 'When did you leave Sweetwater? How's things at home?'

"Jim loved a joke as well as they did. 'You made me ride that cussed mule,' he said. 'Now, dammit, every last one of you boys has to ride him or I'll fire you!' They didn't all do as well as Jim had done, but every single one had to make the attempt at riding that outlaw mule. They decided the joke wasn't on Jim after all."

Bob Wood was also working at the DZ. He said, "One of the famous DZ cowboys was an Englishman. He worked at the ranch for all the years that Jim Newman owned the DZ. He never mentioned his family, nor his past history, but he spoke with an English accent, and was evidently an educated man. Therefore, the men decided that he had committed some crime in England and had to leave the country.

The man had read all the classics, and often quoted Shakespeare or the Bible. Usually quiet and self-effacing in a crowd, he had a fiery temper, and could become eloquent when frustrated in what he tried to do. Bob Wood loved to tell about what the Englishman said when he found he couldn't catch a frisky horse:

"He tried three or four times to put the bridle on the horse, but each time the mount would jerk away, run a little, stop till he would reach out to hold him, then run again. Finally, he threw the bridle on the ground, threw his hat on top of it, then jumped up and down on top of both of them. He shook his fist and yelled in his British accent, 'God made Man in his own image. He made him Master of all the fish in the sea, and of all the beasts in the field. His job was to boss all this livestock, and I, the poor, weak, little fool, can't even outrun a frisky pony!'"[106]

Even the boss's wife wasn't immune to being the butt of a joke. Ora Wood of the H-Bar Ranch said, "The boys loved a joke better than anything. There was a one-legged cowboy they called 'Timber,' because of his wooden leg. I called him 'Mr. Timber' for months, and they never told me that wasn't his real name. It finally dawned on me that 'Timber' was only a nickname, but the boys had a good laugh on me in the meantime."[107]

Bob Wood told of an incident that happened while he was foreman of the H-Bar Ranch: A newly hired cowboy suffered the brunt of many jokes. Once at a branding, the cowboys had gotten hold of some ice, possibly from hail. They grabbed the tenderfoot and told him that they were going to brand him.

He didn't believe them, so wasn't too worried. But the boys hog-tied the man, pulled the red-hot branding iron out of the fire, pressed the ice against his rump, and held a piece of bacon against the branding iron until it sizzled. Between the feel of the ice and the sound and smell of the sizzling meat, the man believed he really had been branded and screamed to high heaven. The relief of finding out that he had not actually been

---

[106] Bob Wood. interview by Rose White. 1932.

[107] Ora Wood. interview. 1932

branded was not enough to keep him from being angry at his companions the rest of the day.

For the most part, cowboys on the plains got along well together and depended upon each other. In an unsettled country where people were far away from civilization, it was important to be able to work together and to make no enemies when one's life might depend on his companions.

Lonny Horn

Lonny Horn, owner of the Pigpen Ranch. Harold Kilmer & Don McAlavy. *High Plains History Book. 1980.*

James "Buster" DeGraftenreid on right with unknown cowboy. Courtesy of ENMU Golden Library Special Collections.

Chapter 22
Buster DeGraftenreid at the Pigpen

J.E. "Buster" DeGraftenreid, one of the most colorful of the early setttlers on the Llano Estacado, was born in Grayson County, Texas on the family plantation in September of 1864. He was a nephew of famous lawman, John Selman. The family migrated to New Mexico in the early 1880s, and in 1882, Buster went to work for the Causey Brothers hunting buffalo.[108]

Buster said, "I was about 14 years old and in November 1883, I worked for George Causey in his Buffalo camp north of Yellow House Canyon. He, Causey, had sold his water right at Yellow House to Jim Newman in 1881.

"George Causey was the last buffalo hunter on the plains. He had a big freight outfit of oxen; freighted from Las Vegas and Fort Worth. He told me his was the first wagons that crossed the plains. In 1879 he had loaded at Ft. Worth for a rangers outfit on Cat Fish Creek that was on the East side.

"He then hunted and killed buffalo at Yellow House and in the spring of 1879 loaded his hides and meat, seven wagons with trailer wagons and seven to eight yokes of steer to a wagon. He said he had made the trip horseback and knew the way from Yellow House to Silver Lake to Salt Lake to Portales Lake to Tierra Blanca to Big Tules; from Tules to Stinking Spring to Tiaban to Ft. Sumner up the Pecos to Las Vegas.

"You see the big cattle herds couldn't cross the plains only in a rainy season when there was rain water in the lakes. After George Causey went from the Yellow House to Ft. Sumner with

---

[108] Dee Blythe. "Melrose Pioneer Once Traded Horses With Geronimo." *Clovis Evening News* .May 31, 1937.

his big bull team, he made such a plain road people began to cross the plains."[109]

After the buffalo hunting was no longer profitable, Buster worked for several outfits in New Mexico and Texas. In 1893 he went to work for Lonnie Horn at the Pigpen Ranch. Lucien Maxwell had purchased the old buildings at Ft. Sumner when the Indians confined there were permitted to return to their reservations. He maintained a 36,000 acre ranch until 1882, when it was purchased and divided by four men: Lonnie Horn, Sam Doss, D. L. Taylor, and John Lord.

Horn located his ranch, called the Pigpen because of the distinctive "#" brand, at the Tules south of the present town of Melrose. The ranch house was built of adobe in an "L" shape with floor joists, windows, ceiling beams, and so forth, all torn out and hauled from the old Maxwell house where Billy the Kid was killed.[110]

The Tules were two lakes, the Big and Little Tules, named for the tules or reeds that grew in them. They were originally called *Las Cañadas*, meaning the reeds; and *Las Cañaditas* will be found listed as such on the old maps.

Buster told of his experiences at the Pigpen: "I think it was in 1893, I was working for the Pig Pen, and there was so many cattle on the Pecos River, there wasn't any grass. I was wagon boss. Mr. Lonny Horn, the owner, lived in Denver, Colorado; he finally come down to Ft. Sumner. After seeing the conditions, he told me to go ahead and do the best I could, as they was all going to die anyway. There wasn't anything at The Tulies, as those lakes was called in them days. The LFD's and Phelps White were at Tierra Blanca, east and south.

"So I got me some Mexicans and come out to those lakes and made tanks and ditches for the water to run in and made plenty water. The old grass was good out there as there wasn't any cattle closer than 15 miles.

"By the time I got the water fixed, my horses were fat. I went back to the Pecos; the fall round-up was working up from

[109] Buster DeGraftenreid. letter to Rose White. January 11, 1940.

[110] "History of the Pig Pen Ranch." *YourPaper*, March 1982.

Roswell. I gathered the Pigpen cattle and my own and several little men's cattle, about 2,500 head in all. They was pore.

"That was December 18, 1893. All the men was anxious to quit so they would be in Ft. Sumner by Christmas, so myself and one Mexican boy, one of old Salidon Trujillo's boys stayed there. There wasn't a house or nothing. About five miles south on the hard land was lots of mesquite roots that we got for wood when we had time. When the grass wasn't good to stake our night horses, we would move our camp to better grass."

Buster continued, "It was 40 miles to Ft. Sumner, and when we got out of tobacco and cartridges, one of us would go in with a pack horse and bring back what groceries we had to have. It taken a day to go, a day to learn the news, and a day to come back. Maybe you think the one who stayed home wasn't glad when he came home with all kind of news and lots of papers, a month old, but all news to us.

"We rode line south of the cattle every day, and if it was storming stayed with them until the storm was over; maybe all day and night. Then start them back and they would come on in to water. In the spring, in April, we lost maybe 75 head. They wintered good as grass was knee-deep everywhere.

"The second winter we dug a dugout and sure had a good house. Then I built a big six-room adobe, or had it built in 1888, and Mr. Horn moved from Denver, Colorado.

"In 1899 I left the ranch and went to Texas. Moved back and went to work again in 1902 and what a change there was in every way. The nesters was coming and HELL broke loose when the railroad got from Texico to Belen."[111]

---

[111] DeGraftenreid. letter to Rose White. January 24, 1940.

Urton Family. W. G. Urton, son B. W. , Mrs. Urton, and standing
in front, W. C. "Cooley" Urton. Courtesy *New Mexico Stockman.*
1949.

Chapter 23
Cooley Urton and the Bar-V

W. C. "Cooley" Urton and his brother, B. W. "Ben" came to the High Plains with their parents when they were small boys. The Urtons were part of the group known as the "Missourians," who established a ranch at Cedar Creek on the east side of the Pecos River, sixty miles northeast of the present town of Roswell. These men, W. G. Urton, Lee Easley, J. D. Cooley, Ben Duncan, Perry Craig, Harvey Russell, William Meyers, and John C. Knorp left Cass County, Missouri in 1884 for the Pecos country, and established the 7HL Ranch, later the Bar-V.

Unlike the ranches further east on the Llano Estacado, the Urton family had plenty of water, but they suffered from other hardships common to their neighbors to the east: no schools, churches, or other home comforts. Attacks by rustlers and Indians, though infrequent, caused havoc, but entertained the two small boys immensely.

Supplies were trailed from Las Vegas, New Mexico, but were often received months after they were expected. The mail came from Ft. Stanton and was also undependable; the letter notifying Mr Urton Sr. of his mother's demise arrived three weeks after her death.

Medical care could not be depended upon. Once a messenger was sent to Roswell on a Friday for Dr. E. H. Skipwith to attend son Ben who had the measles. Dr. Skipwith didn't arrive until the following Sunday noon, saying he knew the boy would be well or dead, so he had taken his time.[112]

When one of the Bar-V punchers suffered a broken leg in a fall from his horse, his leg was broken below the knee and the

---

[112] Georgia B. Redfield. "W.G. Urton." *WPA Federal Writer's Project.* January 20, 1939.

bone was split. The doctor couldn't come from Roswell, so one of the cowboys used whiskey as an anaesthetic and proceeded to set the broken bone. By spring the injured leg was three inches shorter than the other, but the doctor said that nothing could be done unless the bones were re-broken. That was a harsh verdict for the puncher, so he decided to leave well enough alone.[113]

Jack Potter regarded the Urtons as dependable historians: "I can remember you asking if I knew a Mr. Urton. Yes, I knew he and his brother Cooley at Roswell. They were boys that came to Pecos with their father late in 1884 or early 1885. I find him to be the best historian on the Pecos.

"Cooley and Ben his brother that passed on, they were white or red-headed boys when the big cattle rush was on in the early and middle 1889s, while visiting around the old bunk house and listening to cowboys tell their yarns, and some times got down to facts. Often while old Uncle Jim Chisum was on his way to Las Vegas in his buckboard, he would stay all night at their father's Company Ranch. Uncle Jim would set up til midnight telling about the Chisum Jingle-bobs and the claim he had against the Indian department for stolen stock. All this stuff soaked in, and fifty or sixty years later they are able to put out just as they heard it."[114]

The Urtons knew many of the old timers who made history in the early days. They were acquainted with the Indian lady Deluvina, who was known as a good friend of Billy the Kid and was the only person who would enter the room of Pete Maxwell to see if Billy was dead after Pat Garrett shot at him.

Cooley said, "I knew Delavinia [sic] when I was a small boy. She lived with a family close to our ranch and was a frequent visitor. I heard her tell my mother about being the one to enter the room to see if Billy was really dead. She spoke of Pete Maxwell as 'Bro. Peet,' as she was raised by Peet's folks."[115]

---

[113] "Bad Men, Woes of Pecos Ranchers Are Discussed." *Clovis News-Journal.* September 23, 1945.

[114] Jack Potter. letter to Rose White.1942.

[115] Cooley Urton. letters to Rose White.1940-1950.

    There were always a number of cowboys who were called by new names, selected by themselves, when they came to the new clean country, where they wished to start with a slate wiped clean. According to the well-known tradition of the West, no questions were ever asked.

    "One of these men was Joe Boren, also known as 'Charley Avery,' and sometimes by the name of 'Pecos,'" said Col. Potter. "He was a little bow-legged fellow; he was in a fight near Seymour, Texas. He was called 'Charley Very' by the cowboys."

    Joe Boren, aka Charley Avery worked for the DZ and other ranches, among them the Bar-V. Cooley Urton knew him well, and had this to say about him: "Once Charley was caught in a snow storm and was forced to stay on the open prairie for three days. He managed to build a little fire and keep it going and he killed a rabbit or two and ate them; but his horse froze to death. So he had to walk ten miles to the ranch house; not much the worse for wear. But in a few weeks his gray hair all fell out and when it came back in it was all black. He was a tough little guy; never did tell his real name until he 'heired' some money back east and had to go and claim it."

    Cooley continued, "Charlie Avery was working for the Cattle Inspection Board, when he was sent to Clayton to inspect some cattle that were being sent to Montana. It was tho't some stolen cattle were among them. The dishonest ranchers knew that they could not put anything over on Charley when he was sober, so they got him drunk, and when the cattle were shipped; he was too drunk to look them over.

    "But Charlie was a hard-headed little man and when he sobered up, he realized what had happened. So he got on a train and went to Montana. When the cattle arrived, Charlie was already there. He looked them over, and told which ones should be cut out because they had been stolen. As a result of this, two or three ranchers around Clayton were indicted for cattle stealing. When the time came for the trial, a summons was sent to my father's ranch for Charley, but he was way up in the mountains; and by the time a man rode up to get him, it was too late for him to get to Springer in time for the trial.

"The judge was going to have Charlie put in jail for failing to appear, but my father went up and talked to the judge and got him to set a new date for the trial. 'Will you guarantee he'll be here next time?' said the Judge. 'Yes, if you'll give me ten days to find him in after I get the papers.' So Charlie got another chance and next time he was in Springer on time and testified against the cattle thieves. He made a very fast ride and got there on time."

Cooley and his family were acquainted with Black Jack Ketchum and his gang who were notorious for robbing trains: "I knew the Ketchum brothers and some others of the gang. The Ketchums worked at the Bar V Ranch two seasons while I was there. They stole horses from the ranch and were riding some of them at the robbery when Sam was wounded. Some of the horses were killed or wounded in the fight after they had robbed the train. Only one horse was unharmed and horses were too cheap to go for him."

Col. Potter also knew the outlaw: "Black Jack Ketchum was a good cowman. He would tail-up cows, a practice of getting cows on their feet when they got bogged down in mud or snow or were too weak to stand by themselves. He had lots of patience. Later he got to robbing trains. Folsom was where they robbed them. This time they could not uncouple the express car from the rest of the train and the conductor came along and shot B.J. in the arm and in the side.

"He was taken to Trinidad where his arm had to be amputated. He spent 18 months in jails and penitentiaries, then they decided he must be hanged. When they hung him, the fall jerked his head off. They sewed it back on and buried him. Thirty-two years later they decided to move the bodies in our 'Boot Hill Cemetery.' About 1500 people gathered. When they lifted Black Jack Ketchum's coffin out, an Oxford shoe was the first thing we saw. A reporter standing by me said, 'Black Jack Ketchum! Boot Hill Cemetery! You must have dug up the wrong man!' Very humiliatin' to us old-timers, that shoe. I said, 'It's Black Jack all right. See, his sleeve is sewed up, and you can see his black mustache.' It turned out the jailer had taken his boots and put Oxford shoes on him instead."

Cooley wrote several articles for newspapers and magazines. His article, "Roundup on the Pecos," published in the New Mexico Stockman, June 1949, is one of the most highly regarded descriptions of life on the roundup that has ever been written.[116]

In 1889 J. J. Cox, on the ranch adjoining the 7HL, was taken sick and died. His ranch and ranch lands of others who had grown discouraged were bought by the Cass Land and Cattle Company which then became the largest and most important cattle owners on the Pecos River in New Mexico; and the 7HL name was changed to the Bar V Ranch.

---

[116] Cooley Urton. "Roundup on the Pecos." *New Mexico Stockman*. 1949.

Joe Beasley. Courtesy of Jim Warnica.

Chapter 24
Joe Beasley

Joe Beasley was one of the oldest "old-timers" who was still living in Portales in 1937. Rose White interviewed him and wrote of him in that year.[117] Since 1884 his knowledge of the old ranches and of the cowboys who lived on them was at first hand. Although he ranched on the Pecos, his work took him through the Portales Valley at frequent intervals; and his ranching at a later date in Roosevelt County helped to make him one of the real pioneers.

Joe was born in San Saba County, Texas, in 1866. From his earliest childhood until he was sixty-two, his life was spent on ranches. Until he was grown he ranched with his father in San Saba County. At thirteen he made his first trip with a trail herd. In 1884 at the age of eighteen, he started in business for himself. With five hundred cattle under the HRZ brand, he moved to a ranch on the Penasco River. In those days most of Eastern New Mexico was in Lincoln County. No one took out any land papers; just lived where they wished and ran their cattle on the open range.

In 1889 Mr. Beasley married Texanna McDaniel in Kingston, New Mexico. Miss McDaniel had been living with a sister and her father at the mouth of Wills Canyon in the Sacramento Mountains, having moved there in 1887. After their marriage Mr. and Mrs. Besaley ranched in the White Sands area, with their home located just down the road from the modern day entrance to the White Sands Monument. .

Around 1893 a severe drouth affected ranching in the White Sands area, and the Beasley, with one daughter, drove their

---

[117] Joe Beasley. interview by Rose White. 1937.

remaining cattle to Oklahoma and homesteaded near Cheyenne, Oklahoma. Later in 1901 after the passsage of the herd Law in Oklahoma, the Beasleys left and drove their cattle back to New Mexico and wintered on Cibola Draw, south of Ft. Sumner.

In 1902 Joe Beasley homesteaded in the Blackwater Draw, east of Uncle Joe Lang's place near the family of Lee Garrett, in the sandhills fourteen miles northwest of Portales. Joe, having used up his homestead rights in Oklahoma, filed under the name of his brother-in-law, Dallas McDaniel. This place was always known as the McDaniel place.

Having located on this homestead, the Beasleys then moved to town, so that their two daughters could go to school. Their home was on North Main, and Joe Beasley lived there until his death in 1940. He knew all of the old cowmen and punchers; remembered all of them, how they looked, and what they were like.

One thing about Joe, he didn't exaggerate. When he told an old story, you felt sure it was just that way. Too many old timers were inclined to embroider the facts in order to make a good story.

Beasley recalled that, "The DZs were already at Salt Lake in 1884, and Doak Good was at Portales Springs. He had a little adobe house above the Springs. When I was working in the Land Office about 1910, I helped fix the papers whereby Doak was selling his land at Portales Springs; about three hundred acres. At that time, Doak was living in California.

"There were several fights at Portales Springs. Jim Newman and Doak Good emptied their guns at each other just at dawn one morning, but neither was hit. Rube Seekers and Doak also had a fight there."

Joe didn't believe the old story about Jim Newman's shooting twenty-five of Doak's fat steers. He remembered that the steers were shot, but didn't think Newman did it. He also remembered clearly the time when Jim Hysaw, who at the time worked on the DZ Ranch, and Sheriff Dan Allan from Lincoln County had a gun fight.

He reported, "Doak Good and me and Jim was there at Doak's house when this sheriff from Lincoln County comes up and Doak introduces him to Jim Hysaw. Well, it turnes out that he had come up there hunting Jim, who was wanted on a charge of cattle stealin.' But when the sheriff tries to arrest him, Jim starts shootin'. The sheriff gets out his gun and starts shootin' too, but neither one hurts the other. The sheriff goes back without his man, though."

Joe Beaseley knew the famous Pat Garrett well. Of him, he said, "He was all right of his kind; but I don't like the kind. Always poppin' off; telling what a bad man he was."

He remembered all the old DZ cowboys: Charley Avery, Jim Warren, Caleb Giles, Bob Wood, Sid Boykin, Jim Stone and many others. He had a good word for all of them.

The cowmen must have liked Joe. A man so quiet and friendly and unassuming must have been a favorite with all of them. Contrary to general practice in those wild times, he never drank nor smoked. Perhaps that is one reason why he always had an outfit of his own. Jim Stone and Sid Boykin were two more who were always sober and managed to be successful.

Joe's daughter Verda married Jim Warnica who had come to Eastern New Mexico in 1900 along with his brother Frank and family. Joe died in 1940 and is buried in Portales alongside his wife, mother-in-law and brother-in-law.[118]

Jim and Verda Warnica had two children, Jim Jr. and Gladys Lee. Jim Jr. is well-respected as an archeologist and has published several studies on the archeology of Blackwater Draw and the Portales Valley.

---

[118] Jim Warnica. letter to Ruth Burns. 2011.

Old-time cowhands. Jim Wiggins. Lon Reed. R. E. L. White.
Ft. Sumner. 1886. Burns Collection.

Chapter 25
Other Cowboys

There were many cowboys who have quietly faded into the background in stories of the early days in the west. In interviews and letters, they are mentioned in stories and accounts of incidents, sometimes by only a sentence.

The names of these men appear in other writings, in books, in genealogies, and so forth. It is important to mention their names and the things that were said about them by the eye-witnesses to the events.

Jack Potter recalled, "*Bill Linch* was a schemer. He sold an English a worthless tract of land near Las Vegas, covered with that worthless broom weed. He represented it as wild alfalfa. I was at the big XIT celebration at Dalhart and there seemed to be a mixed-up on the early history of that big company. I can remember part of the people that was ordered off their holding including Jim Newman, Bill Linch, the big Carter family that located at Tierra Blanca, and *Bennett Howel* that located at Cabra Springs near Las Vegas, and others.[119]

J. E. Brown, Sid Boykin, Caleb Giles, Jim Warren were DZ Newman punchers. Different noted cowboys were in charge at different times; *Henry Mason, Jim Hysaw*, and others.

According to McFatter: "Yes, Jim Hysaw was a rounder and a bad man. Newman seemed to cater to bad men for help. Harry Blocker was his foreman for a while.

"It seems that the best foreman, that was honest and would get along with his neighbors was *John Scott*. In 1878 and 1879 he crossed the plains going to Tascosa and at one time he

---

[119] Potter. Letter. August 18, 1947.

rounded up herd of cattle at Portales Spring and trailed them to Fort Stanton.

Henry Mason was a nice fellow. Was around Portales. *Jim Hysaw* stole a lot of cattle."

"*Buck Richardson* was an old DZ man, lived north of Tucumcari. Never did do any good. *John Scott,* DZ foreman was a good man. Was kin to *Jim Brown,* who married *Lilly Stone.*

"In 1880 when the cattle companies suspected that the Kid was driving off their cattle, they sent *Frank Stewart,* a cowboy with a mount of horses, to go to Chisum range on the Pecos and see if there was Texas cattle over there. Stewart stayed with the Kid's outlaw bunch at Portales Spring. Stewart posed as a common cowhand and stayed only one night."

Lizzie Boykin said, "*Christy* was the Negro cook for Sid's outfit when he moved. They called him '*Big Bell.*'" One time years later Christy saw Mrs. Boykin in Clovis and introduced himself. "I'm Christy; I used to work for Sid." Mrs. Boykin said "I never heard of you." When he told her his nick-name, was Big Bell, she remembered all about him.

Jim Warren was another cowboy who worked for Sid at busy seasons. He was a very peculiar man; never had a word to say about his past. [120]

L. K. Terrell, familiarly known as "Jack County" by everyone for his fondness for his original home in Jack County, Texas, came to New Mexico in 1894. He worked for the Pigpen Ranch for two years and then for the Horeshoes under the Curtiss Brothers. After working at the DZ for a few years, he moved to Tierra Blanca Ranch in 1898 and made his home there with his family for the next fifty years. Because of him, the lake was familiarly known as "Jack County Lake."[121]

"Terrell's daughter, Willie Hinger, recalled the small spring that fed the lake. It was boxed in and the water piped to a wooden trough where the cattle drank. The area was fenced to

---

[120] Lizzie Boykin. 1940.

[121] Article. "Jack County Terrell Started Riding Ranges Here in 1894." *Portales News Tribune.* 1952

keep lobo wolves, antelope and stray cattle away from the carefully hoarded water."[122]

Jack County remembered, "The first I recall hearing of Portales was in 1898 when a contractor set up a tent city here to build fifty miles of road bed for the Pecos Valley Railroad. Hundreds of men worked out of Portales that year with two-horse scrapers. Saloons and other suppliers were operated from wagons that first year."

W. O. Dunlap Sr. came to the High Plains in 1898 with his family. He moved his home to a new location with a team of mules, and founded the community of Dunlap, thirty-four miles southwest of Ft. Sumner. He acted as a locater for homesteaders seeking a claim. However the town of Dunllap disappeared when the settlers failed to make a living on their claims.

According to his son, W. O. Dunlap Jr., his father made his living as well-driller and house-mover.[123] Mr. Dunlap once worked at the H-Bar Ranch for Bob Wood; and later he worked for *Buffalo Jones* caring for his herd of buffalo. Jones attempted to breed the buffalo with local beef cattle, but the attempt was a failure.[124] Jones also kept a ranch near Portales to train horses and dogs for use in his attempts to rope gorillas and other wild animals and bring them to civilization for study.[125]

[122] Kilmer and McAlavy. (U.S.A. *High Plains History.* 1980) p. 41

[123] W. O. Dunlap Jr. interview by Rose White.

[124]Dunlap. Article. *Portales News-Tribune.*

[125] Easton, Robert and Mackenzie Brown. *Lord of the Beasts.* (Tuscon: University of Arizona Press. 1961) p. 200.

Portales Depot. ENMU Golden Library SpecialCollection

Josh Morrison's Store. 1898.ENMU Special Collections.

Chapter 26
The Railroad: Arrival of the Homesteaders

In 1898 the Pecos Valley and Northeastern Railroad, erected from Amarillo to Roswell, reached the present site of Portales, and the way of life on the Eastern Plains was changed forever.

Up to this time, the prairie had been occupied by several large ranches: the DZ, the T-71, the H-Bar, the Pigpen, the LFD, and a few smaller spreads. There were no trees, other than a few big cottonwoods, which had been brought from Ft. Sumner and planted in the 1880s. The only structures to break the loneliness of the prairie were adobe ranch houses, barns, windmills, and a few scattered half-dugouts serving as line camps. Other than these few ranches, the whole area was one vast plain, populated only by buffalo, antelope and other wild creatures.

Of course these huge ranches did not own all the land they were using. They owned only a small acreage where the house and barns were located, and the rest was free government land. There were no fences and the cattle roamed at will. The cattle stayed fairly well on their own range, but in winter, they would drift before a blizzard and might end up as far south as Monahans, Texas.

In 1898 when the railroad finally reached as far as what is now Roosevelt County, then Chaves County, a great many people began to come and file on claims for homesteads. Real estate companies were quick to seize the opportunity to advertise the new area and attracted many settlers with tales of fertile farm lands and quick profits. Each man or woman was required to build a house within six months and to live on the place for three years. Within ten years, every available homesite near the railroad was taken; and the little town of Portales sprang up to take care of their needs.

Josh Morrison had built a little store at the DZ Ranch at Salt Lake to supply the ranchers with a few necessities. When he saw the opportunity arising from the increased travel via the railroad, he put his little store on skids and dragged it to the townsite of Portales with a pair of mules. He then built a house next door and moved in his wife and sons Seth and Paul. He ordered a stock of staples: canned goods, dried fruit, crackers, and tools, and began a lively trade with the new arrivals and the cowhands who brought their herds to town for shipping on the new railroad.

One of the first comers, Miss Ella Turner, described her arrival in Portales thus, "We came here in 1899, twenty-four of us in five covered wagons and a buggy. We arrived on the first day of May in a typical sandstorm. As if this was not enough, our food had given out, and we had to buy something for our dinner. Well, we stopped our wagons across the road from Mr. Morrison's house, and went over to buy something for dinner.

"We got some cans of things and some crackers; then we asked for stamps. Uncle Josh, (we called him that), replied, 'We don't sell stamps. You have to buy them in Roswell or Hereford.' Then in reply to another question, 'Yes, they put the mail off the train here, and everyone looks it over and takes his own. We put the outgoing mail in a box and the train picks it up. No, we don't have a doctor. I don't know how we get along. We just don't get sick much.'"[126]

To file on a claim, homesteaders had to go to Roswell, the county seat of what was then Chaves County. Miss Turner continued, "We rested a day or so, then four of us decided to go to Roswell and see how we liked the prospect there. People told us that the road was so sandy that they were sure we couldn't get there in our buggy, but we decided to try it anyway. Roswell was then the county seat, and we made up our minds to file on claims, either near there or near Portales. We did finally reach Roswell, though we thought many times that we would never make it, as the road was so sandy. I remember passing J. B. Sledge's ranch on the way. At that time he was living in a dugout.

---

[126] Ella Turner. interview by Rose Whte. 1936.

It was the first dugout I had ever seen, and I remember thinking how strange it looked, with his little dog running around on top.

"We looked around the country at Roswell, but found we liked Portales better, so we filed on our claims, and made the week-long, tiresome journey back. Perhaps the thought of trying to get our heavily-loaded wagons through that dreadful sand helped us to decide on Portales."

Newcomers lived in dugouts or tents or in their wagons until they could build a home. They soon found that lumber had to be hauled in from Ft. Sumner or Amarillo, and was expensive, so most homes were built of sod.

Miss Turner continued, "People kept telling us what a dry country it was, so we thought it was safe to put a sod roof on our houses. Not long after they were finished, an unusually heavy rain fell, and right away the roofs began to leak. The sod just melted away, and water and mud came pouring into the houses. When the rain stopped you may be sure that we put on a different kind of roof."

Some of the newcomers arrived in desperate straits. The family of Grace Scott Henderson had a tragic time of it before coming to Portales. Her father, Mack Scott, had come to New Mexico in search of gold. He had moved from place to place with his family hunting gold; had lived for a time at Santa Rosa, at Cloudcroft, at Hillsboro, and at Weed. Once they were so poor that there was nothing to eat but a box of laundry starch.

Grace told of the death of her little brother Raymond who starved to death: "Mother had to wean him because the twins were coming, and they could not afford to buy milk for him. So she did the best she could, fed him on sugar and bread and water. The poor little thing got sick, as any baby would have done on such a diet. When he became steadily worse, Uncle John walked ahead and carried a lantern while Father drove the wagon to Hillsboro.

"The trip took a day and a half, but little Raymond did not have to stand the jolting so long, for he died on the way."[127]

---

[127] Grace Scott Henderson. interview by Rose White. 1936

Mrs. Henderson told of her arrival in Portales: "When we came to Portales, there wasn't another soul in town but Uncle Josh Morrison, Mrs. Morrison, and their boys, Seth, and Paul. I, along with my father and mother, brothers and sisters, arrived in a covered wagon without a bite to eat. Seth took pity on us and gave us food. My father never forgot it."

She continued, "In Portales, that first winter, the children were without shoes. My mother offered to wash some shirts for some cowboys to get money to buy shoes. The children dressed up in the shirts to play cowboy, before they were washed, and caught the measles from them! My father built a box tent, used his wagon to carry express and freight, and remained in Portales to bring up our family."

Miss Ella Turner reminisced, "When we reached Portales three or four more houses were being built, but none were finished. Then, too, there were several families living in box tents, and a saloon or two. This little collection of buildings made up the whole town of Portales on May 11, 1899.

"Of course people came in fast from then on, for the railroad had reached Portales in the fall of 1898. Inside of a year or two, there was quite a nice little town here, with lots of houses and stores."

Chapter 27
Ranchers vs Nesters

Naturally the ranchers resented the intrusion of the "nesters," as they called the homesteaders, and did all they could to discourage them. The ranchers hated to have their range cut up into farms and did everything possible to make the nesters feel they were fighting a losing battle. Ranchers complained that the homesteaders ruined the virgin grass by plowing, causing the wind to blow all the top soil from these fields. They refused to control their cattle, and were glad when a homesteader gave up and moved back where he had come from.[128]

Tom Trammell, one of Bob Wood's bosses at the H-Bar, told him: "Don't give the nesters a damn thing. Don't loan them anything, don't sell them anything. Don't even give them a cottonwood switch for a tree." [129]

However, one year Miss Ella had a nice little garden, and her brothers were away on a trip to Texas, when a lot of cows got into her garden. She related, "I hurried to town to buy some wire to fix a fence, but was told that there was no wire to be had in town. 'None closer than Amarillo,' said one storekeeper. What should I do? If I waited till wire could be sent from Amarillo, my garden would be ruined. I finally decided to take my courage in my hands and go to Uncle Bob Wood at the H-Bar.

"I knew how the ranchers hated us nesters, but I was desperate. I just couldn't let my garden be ruined. So I drove in my buggy to the H-Bar. Eddie and Bill White, little boys then, came running to open the big wooden gate for me. They always loved to open the gate. Luckily, Mr. Wood was home. He lent me

---

128 Rose White. "A Man Was a Real Man in Them Days." Speech,

129 Bob Wood, interview by Rose White. 1932.

Barbed Wire Fences meant "The End of The Open Range."
Painting by Don McAlavy. Burns Collection.

the wire in spite of strict orders from Trammell against any loans to those 'damn' nesters.

"In a few days, some wire was shipped in and I was able to roll up his wire and return it. I have always been grateful to Mr. Wood for his kindness. Mr. Trammell would have fired him if he had found out about it."[130]

Mrs. Wood often gave her new neighbors starts of multiplier onions and shared buckets of peaches in the fall. Mr. Wood also loaned out grain for a neighbor's horses against strict orders from Newman and Trammell. Sure enough, the neighbor repaid him with grain when the supply wagons came in the fall.

Having the railroad nearby to ship their cattle to market was a big advantage to the ranchers. They no longer had to trail herd their cattle to Dodge City or Hayes City, Kansas. They could ship them out by rail, avoiding the loss of many cattle along the way. Portales became a major shipping point on the Eastern Plains. Sometimes as many as two thousand head would be gathered at the tracks, awaiting shipment.

Miss Ella related, "As it was only a mile to town, we usually walked. I remember that, the first time we walked, we debated as to how to get past the cattle waiting near the railroad to be loaded and shipped to market. We knew that the cowboys hated the nesters, as they called the homesteaders. But we had also heard that the cows, although paying no attention to men on horseback or in wagons, would chase and even attack people on foot.

"My brothers would not ask the cowboys to help us, so I finally plucked up enough courage to ask. The cowboys were real polite, and rode between us and the cows until we were safely past, and did the same thing as we returned from town. They always did this when people walked past their herds. I have counted as many as five large herds of cattle waiting near the railroad to be shipped."

---

[130] Ella Turner. interview by Rose White. 1936.

Chapter 28
Conditions in a New Land

The newcomers found conditions far different from anything they had been led to expect. They had been told by real estate promoters that wonderful crops could be raised on the virgin prairie soil. The promoters failed to mention the drawbacks: the lack of water, the lack of wood, the sweep of sand and wind over unprotected fields, the wild rabbits that ate up tender little plants. Many who came did not have enough money to dig a well or to last through one failure of crops. The wonder is that anyone stayed at all. A great many didn't. They sold their "relinquishments" and moved back to their former homes in Texas, Arkansas, or Oklahoma, leaving behind a trail of rabbit bones, as the rabbits were often the only meat they had on their return journey.

The ones who stayed became the true pioneers of the twentieth century. While Las Vegas, Albuquerque, and Santa Fe were enjoying electricity, running water in the house, and telephones, these poor pioneers found that they had moved to what was marked on early maps as "The Great American Desert."

The farming, at best, was very discouraging. "Farming was a poor business in those days," reminisced Mrs. Ora Wood. "Often, we could not sell our vegetables after we had raised them. Chickens were twenty-five cents apiece, and eggs, ten cents a dozen. Often you could not sell them at any price. One year we had the finest crop of onions you ever saw. But one day the hail hit the onions and simply ruined them. You could smell onions clear into Portales."[131]

---

[131] Ora Wood. interview by Rose White.1932.

When corn was planted in the spring, the high sandy winds cut it down, or the rabbits ate it as fast as the little plants came up. Or the neighboring ranchers let their cattle tramp through the fields, destroying everything as they went. The standard menu for these first families was beans, sourdough biscuits, and coffee. Very seldom was there any meat other than bacon. When there was any, it was usually an XIT steer that had been butchered in the fond hope that it would not be missed; since the cattle were never counted, except for the steers that were to be shipped, or the calves that were branded. Of course there were always rabbits, and once in a while, an antelope; but for months at a time, there would be no meat other than bacon.

At first there was no doctor nearer than Amarillo. Even after Dr. J. S. Pearce came to Portales in 1900, each family kept a medicine shelf stocked with the standard remedies of the day and took care of minor illnesses. Always there was calomel, castor oil, and epsom salts. Mustard plasters were widely used, and coal oil mixed with sugar was considered a good cough syrup. Of course there was no penicillin nor aspirin, but a bottle of whiskey served many purposes. It was used as an antiseptic, as an anesthetic, as a cure for coughs or even for snakebite; and for a general feeling of depression.

In these years of poor crops and little or no ready cash, women found that it was almost impossible to buy any material for sewing, and of course there were practically no store-made women's or girls' clothes. One old-timer, Mrs. Jim Dobbs Burke, remembered, "There were no bolts of material in the local store, except two patterns of calico, one red, and one blue. The consequence was that all the little girls had dresses of one bolt or the other, red or blue.

"For making underwear, the women used flour sacks. There was one difficulty: no matter what method was used, the printing could not be removed. It would not rub out, boil out, nor fade out. Therefore, many nice women wore panties, tucked and ruffled though they might be, with 'MOSES BEST' printed in big black letters across the seat."[132]

---

[132] Mrs. Jim Dobbs Burke. interview by Rose White. 1940.

Inside a prairie home. Courtesy ENMU Golden Library
Special Collections.

Chapter 29
Scarcity of wood and water

The homesteaders who were not prosperous enough to drill their own wells had to haul water in barrels from a neighbor's well, sometimes as far away as six or even eight miles. They found that there were no trees or bushes to provide wood for building houses, or even for fires. And so, of necessity, the first homes were dugouts or half-dugouts. The roof might be of boards, and the front might have one window and a door. The lumber had to be shipped from Amarillo, and was very expensive. Until the house was finished, the family lived in the covered wagon, and the mother cooked over an open fire.

Mrs. Annie King Greaves told of her arrival on the plains in her memoir, *Six Miles to The Windmill*. Her husband was away hauling supplies when someone dropped her and her baby off at the new homesite: "Can you see yourself, a twenty-three year old girl with a six-month old baby standing and seeing the only other living being drive off, knowing there wasn't a human in at least three miles in one direction and in perhaps a hundred in the other?

"I turned and went down into the house. 'Down into' is right. The eight steps went from the level of the ground to the dirt floor of the house. The walls of the house were seven feet high; four feet in the ground and three above. Outside the eaves of the house didn't come to your waist line. The door was at one end of the 15x30 room, with a window opposite the door. Since the walls on the sides above the ground were not high enough for a window set upright, one on each side was set in sideways and instead of raising, you pushed the window sideways."[133]

---

[133] Annie King Greaves. *Six Miles to the WIndmill.* (Portales: 1976) p. 13.

In the first day of their arrival, the homesteaders found that cow chips were the only available fuel. Many women were shocked to find that they had to cook with them; but it was either that or eat the food raw, so they soon became accustomed to them. If there was any spare time, the whole family wandered over the prairie, dragging tow sacks, collecting fuel for the next day's cooking. The cow chips were all right for a quick meal, say, biscuits and fried potatoes and bacon; but they burned out quickly, leaving a stove full of ashes. If the men had time, they dug mesquite roots which burned slowly and made a more lasting fire.

In winter, with so little fuel, it was hard to keep warm. Sometimes, in the fall, a group of men would go in wagons to the "brakes" near Tucumcari and bring back loads of wood. Even then, real cold weather meant that the whole family would often stay in bed to keep warm.

Mrs. Ruth McCowen of Elida has said that when she was a girl, she and her father lived on a claim near the Organ Mountains. One evening, a rancher arrived at their place, and asked permission to water his large herd of cattle and to stay all night. Her father said that would be just fine, and he and his daughter started toward the house. Then Mrs. McGowen said, "Papa, why on earth did you tell that man he could stay with all those cattle? Just think what a mess of manure there will be round the windmill." To which the father replied, "Yes, but just think how much good fuel we will have next winter." [134]

Mr. J. G. Greaves, father of Gordon Greaves and a former editor of the Portales News-Tribune, has written, "It took two days a week to pick up cow chips, and one day to haul household water. This left only four days for farming."[135]

The scarcity of water was an ever-present worry to the housewife. Three barrels had to do for a week, and this meant for washing, mopping, bathing, and for cooking and drinking. Not a cupful, not a drop was wasted. Boys were soundly thrashed for

---

[134] Ruth McGowen. interview with Rose White. 1936.

[135] J. G. Greaves. Article. *Portales News-Tribune.*

engaging in water fights. Dish water was poured on some little plant or rosebush, as was also bath water or wash water.

On wash day, a big iron pot was set up in the yard, filled with the precious water, and a fire built under it. The water was used over and over: first for the white clothes, then for the light-colored ones, then the dark-colored, then the men's dirty pants and shirts. The rinse water was treated to the same hard use. Wash Day was a regular Monday affair, and lasted all day, with only time for a meager supper of leftovers.

Saturday night was bath night, with the whole family cleaning up. If water was very scarce, the whole family used the same water, beginning with the cleanest one. One would think this was not true, though it stood to reason it would be so; but a school teacher who was staying with a pioneer family in the early 1900s wrote of her experience. On Saturday night, the mother said to her, "The children and I have had our baths, so now you can take yours; but don't pour out the water, because Pa still has to take his."[136]

After the fields had been plowed, another worry arose: the sand began to blow. The plains were always very windy because of the sweep of open country; and the blowing sand made life miserable for everybody, even the ones who stayed in the house; since the sand filtered into everything, even the food. Portales people still talk of the Thanksgiving Day when the air was so full of sand that dinner had to be eaten with newspapers covering the table, and people reaching under to help themselves to the food.

One generous custom of ranch days lasted over into homestead history, and was the nicest feature of this dreary existence. This was the hospitality which demanded that anyone reaching a house at night was welcome to stay and eat and spend the night. No pay was offered, and none would have been accepted if it had been. The payment took the form of news and gossip, which was better than money to lonely people on the plains.

---

[136] Rose White. "Portales in the 1880s."

If travelers arrived at a home to find no one there, it was perfectly all right to go in and sleep, cook meals, and go on your way, without even leaving a note to say anyone had been there. There was only one proviso: the traveler had better clean up his dishes, sweep the floor, make the bed, and leave everything as neat as he found it. To do otherwise made him an outcast from the company of decent men.

Of course these people could not live for years on the money that their dry-land crops produced. The men soon found that they had to take jobs in order to pay for the things they needed. Some of them worked as cowboys for the ranchers; some worked for the railroad; some hauled supplies for the local stores. One man killed cottontail rabbits and shipped them to Denver, where they sold for ten cents apiece.

One homesteader managed to buy a sorghum mill, and ground cane to make syrup which he sold to his neighbors. Mr. Donald Gordon set up a corn grinder, with which he ground corn into meal for his neighbors, taking some of the meal for his pay. The cash that was earned went to buy a cow or a pig, or to buy lumber for a better house. Often the money would be used to pay for drilling a well, thus saving the weekly trips to haul water.

In discussing the many difficulties encountered by the nesters, Gordon Greaves has said, "It was a grim, searing experience for many of them, in which they fought hunger and cold, drought, and the frustrating absence of markets for their produce. It was one of our governments worst blunders, to entice families out on these plains and lead them to expect they could make a living on 160 acres of dry land."[137]

Many homesteaders found it so difficult to survive that they sold their relinquishments and went back east. Those who stayed and braved drought, prairie fires, harsh winds, and hard times, became the founders of a prosperous town.

In the old days when asked why she and her family didn't pack up and leave, Ora Wood would reply, "Cain't, wagon's broke." The truth was that they were too hard up to

---

[137] Gordon Greaves. "By the Way." *Portales News-Tribune. May 15, 1962.*

move anywhere else and so they "just lived pore and did without until they could get another start."

Typical wooden shack. ENMU Golden Library Special Collections.

Dr. J. S. Pearce. Courtesy of ENMU Golden Library Special
Collections.

Chapter 30
Dr. J. S. Pearce: Dedicated Physician

Dr. John Sidney Pearce was born on a plantation in Athens, Louisiana, on February 27, 1886. Dr. Pearce received his medical degree at Tulane University and did his internship at Johns Hopkins. Upon graduation, his first office was at Ringo, Louisiana. One of his first patients was the mother of the future governor of Louisiana at the birth of her son. He was named Huey Pierce Long after the attending physician. Dr. Pearce kept the hand-held scale with which he weighed Huey Long, and used it for weighing the babies in Roosevelt County. It now belongs to James White of Las Cruces, who was attended at his birth by Dr. Pearce.

Dr. Pearce and his family came to Portales in 1899 in a horse and buggy. He had been recruited by the Roswell Chamber of Commerce to practice medicine in that city. He passed through Portales on the way, and after inspecting Roswell, decided that the prospects were more favorable in Portales, and returned there.

Dr. Pearce and C. M. Dobbs went into business together and built an adobe building next to the present Portales News-Tribune office and opened the Pearce and Dobbs Mercantile Store. They also operated a butcher shop; and, as a child, I was shown the dirt cellar under the floor boards which was used for keeping meat cool.

According to Dr. Pearce's granddaughter, Marjorie Linna Gunn, his practice covered all the area from Roswell to Hereford. Settlers on far-flung ranches would keep fresh horses and hot coffee on hand for Dr. Pearce as he traveled to distant homes to tend the sick and injured.[138]

In the 1930s Dr. Pearce still had his office at the rear of the drugstore next to the newspaper office. I well remember the high bed on which he examined patients and the shelves which held all his drugs and oinments. He crushed and mixed his own powders with a mortar and pestle and dispensed them in little folded papers. Liquid medicines were poured into bottles, corked, and labeled with his name and the hand-written name and dosage of the medicine.

In a statement to a patient, Bryan J. Moore, as late as March 3, 1922, Dr. Pearce charged only a minimum, as follows:

3 visits @2.00 ea.		6.00
5 Office treatments	@ 1.00	5.00
Cotton		.40
Tape		.25
2 RX		1.40
Salve		.75
4 RX		3.15
Total		16.95

One of his most trying times was the epidemic of 1918 when so many people were sick and dying of the flu. His wife died from complications of the flu on February 11, 1918. It was said that Dr. Pearce delivered 6,000 babies over his career, none of them in a hospital. He died on March 6. 1941.[139]

---

[138] Marjorie Gunn. Speech to Roosevelt County Historical Society. 1990.

[139] Obituary. *Portales Daily-News.March, 1941.*

Chapter 31
Governor W. E. Lindsey Family

W. E. Lindsey and his wife Amanda came to Eastern New Mexico from Chicago in 1900, trying to find a more healthful climate for Mrs. Lindsey. With them came their two children, Howard and Helen. Mr. Lindsey had practiced law in Chicago for ten years before leaving for the West.

Helen said of their coming: "We first stopped in Colorado and then come on up to Roswell, New Mexico, but the water was so bad there that when Papa came a few months later, he was looking for another location. He come up to Portales on the train and found that the water was so good here that he brought the family on the train to Portales, and that was September of 1900.

"The grass was real high all over everywhere and there were six saloons and two wagon yards in Portales and a few houses. Papa began to practice his legal profession. He had a little office over by the depot, over by the railroad, just a real small office. But at first we just nearly starved to death.

"There wasn't much business and Papa was just about ready to go somewhere else, when the Government filing opened up. Since Papa was U.S. Commissioner, he filed for all these people who came in looking for farms, 160 acres or 320 or 640; and that kept him real busy and from then on everything went quite a bit better.

"My father secured 160 acres of land close to Portales, close to town on a relinquishment. Someone had filed on the land but for some reason wasn't able to live on it the necessary length of time in order to 'prove up' on it, so they sold out. Papa bought this land, and he built our home there and all the children grew up in that home. The house is still standing at 1201 N. Boston Street.

"We raised fruit, cherries, tomatos, and we experimented with cotton. We had a large tank that we watered our yard with, and what was called a 'well-house.' The water from the windmill ran through the well-house and through cement containers there, and we could set our milk on bricks in the water, and as the water went by, it cooled the milk. Then the water went on through the well house and into the tank. The tank we used to water the garden; and then in the winter time, we'd skate on the ice on the tank.

"Mama gave us lots of parties. Mama made lots of taffy and everyone pulled taffy; it was a taffy-pull; we had lots of fun. Then Mama would give quite often a 'watermelon feed,' when the watermelons were all ripe. She'd invite lots of people and everybody would have watermeon and visit and have a good time.

"In the old days, there were so many prairie fires. We'd look out the window almost any time of the day or night and could see fires burning in the distance, and smoke! And then in the winter when the wind blew, oh it would just howl through the windows! We had a couple of loose windows on the north side and to this day I can hear that wind whistling through those windows, it was so cold."

Helen recalled that the saloons burned when the town voted out liquor: "My father was mayor when the town voted out the saloons, and the saloons burned, one after another, about two o'clock in the morning. They were collecting on their insurance; they burned their stock. They burned late at night or early in the morning so there wouldn't be too many people around to fight the fires.

"The way they announced the fires in those days, somebody shot a pistol six times, so everybody came down to fight the fire; and there was a bucket brigade. Papa went on down to fight the fire and Mama hitched up our old white horse to the buggy and it had a place in the back kind of like a pick-up in a way. It had a place in the back to carry things and she put the kerosene stove in the back, and brought it down and set it up in the street there and made coffee for the firefighters.

"The buildings did burn down beause the bucket brigade wasn't able to make much of an impression on the fire."[140]

The Lindseys were very active in the new little community. They helped organize the Presbyterian Church, and Amanda was instrumental in forming the Portales Library and the Cemetary Association. Mr. Lindsey was the first Mayor of Portales and at the Constitutional Convention, he was active in securing funding for the future university. He promoted irrigation and was on the school board, causing the new school to be named "Lindsey School" after him. In 1918 he was elected Lieutenent-Governor of the state of New Mexico, and became Governor when Governor De Baca died. Lindsey died April 5, 1926.

Helen married Lacy Armstrong. She was postmistress for many years and formed an Insurance Company upon her retirement from the post office.

---

[140]Helen Lindsey Armstrong. Interview by Mike Burns Jr., 1973.

Governor W. E. Lindsey. Courtesy of ENMU Golden Library
Special Collections.

Chapter 32
Mattie Lang Mitchell and Sheriff Joe Lang

The Lang and Mitchell families came together to Eastern New Mexico from Texas before the railroad reached Portales.

Mattie Lang Mitchell came on horseback. She said, "My father Joe Lang was here before the railroad came. I came with the cattle, before the family came. Charlie Mitchell, my husband, Tom Jones, the cook, Johnny Milligan, Albert Milligan, and Jim Maguire came then. We brought 1,500 mother cows. The family came the following May or June."[141]

The Lang children were Mattie, Josie, Pearl, Hazel, Bess, and brother Joe Jr. They filed on a homestead twenty miles northwest of Portales. Mattie later married Charlie Mitchell and Pearl married Paul Morrison, son of Josh Morrison, the first resident of Portales. Charlie Mitchell was later one of the early day County Clerks and Mattie was his deputy.

Mattie remembered that a Mrs. Seymour was the teacher of the first union Sunday School which was held in the depot.

As a young woman in Portales and after her marriage, Mattie was often called on to "lay out" the bodies of women and children of those early days. There was no mortician in the little western town at the time, and the men would dig the grave while the women prepared the body.

Joe Lang became the first elected sheriff of the new little town of Portales after Billy Odom's un-official term. He also carried papers as deputy under the sheriff at Amarillo for years. Thus the Lang and Mitchell families were often close observers of

---

[141] Mattie Lang MItchell Carr. interview by Rose White. 1936.

the few killings and other violations of the law that occurred in the surrounding territory.

The families were right in the midst of the area's most well-known fracas: the Spikes Killing that occurred between the Spikes family and Sam Gholson.

Mattie Mitchell told of the killing: "Me and Charlie lived under the Breaks at the time of the Spikes killing. We were right in the middle of it. There were lots of bandits around there. They, the posse [led by Gholson], told my husband Charlie Mitchell they were rounding up the bandits. Charlie and I got in a buggy and came to Portales to be out of the trouble. Gholson was after the Spikes boys. Everyone branded calves without mothers found on their land, just like the Spikes boys did. Gholson got a bunch of men to go with him and killed the Spikes boys. One boy, wounded, crawled eight miles to get help. No one had the nerve to follow. The Spikes boys lived fifteen miles from us.

"Old Man Gholson was part Indian. After he killed these men, he built himself a rock house with windows up high, he was so afraid. He would not let strangers come around, ordered them to leave, would have killed them if they hadn't left in a hurry.

"A few days before the killing Fred Spikes came by our place. He was about twenty-two. When they had a dance, they would always invite Gholson. All were very friendly. We lived three miles from Gholson. My brother had a shooting scrape with them.

"The three Spikes boys were going to build fence when Gholson and his gang ambushed them. They were near a dry arroyo with a little bridge over it. The men hid there. One boy fell behind the embankment. He crawled eight miles to a Mexican's house. He was taken to Hereford, then to Amarillo. Later he was taken to Kansas City. He was two years in the hospitals."

Eddie White was a boy of eleven living at the H-Bar at the time. He said this: "Gholson and John White came to the H-Bar after the killing of the Spikes boys. I remember it just as plain as if it was yesterday. They had the first steel-jacket bullets we had ever seen. The bullets would go through a thick post as clean as could be. John White had a 30-30 rifle and Gholson had a bigger gun. I remember them arguing over which one had shot the bullet that lodged in the cantle of the saddle of one of the Spikes boys. Each one claimed it came from his gun. They talked about the killing, told all about it."[142]

Ora Wood added, "John White was a distant kin of Bob Wood. He came by the H-Bar as he left the country. He told how Gholson paid him to help kill the Spikes boys. Later he tried to blackmail Pa to keep him quiet."[143]

Harold Kilmer and Don McAlavy have a detailed write-up of this killing in the "High Plains History Book."[144]

Another killing was described by Joe Lang's daughter Pearl Morrison: "The first murder trial in Portales was after Doss Boykin killed Henry Stoltz over Henry's wife. Stoltz went to Boykin's house to confront him and was shot, reportedly through a crack in the door.

"After Doss was jailed, his wife Callie passed notes to him in the collar of a shirt. She washed the clothes, and slipped the notes in the ironed shirts.

"Boykin broke out of jail and hid. This was the only jail break while Pa was sheriff. Lizzie Boykin was the cause of him finding Doss. Lizzie told me and I told Pa. I told Pa he was hiding at Jim Bogard's house. He had ridden off on Tom Carraway's black horse. Pa found him and brought him back."[145]

Mattie Lang Mitchell Carr moved to Texas after the death of her husband, Charlie, but came back years later to marry Mr. G. W. Carr, a local lumberman. She died in December of 1961, and Mr. Carr died in 1962. [146]

---

[142] Eddie White. interview. 1940..

[143] Ora Wood. interview. 1932..

[144] Harold Kilmer & Don McAlavy. (U.S.A.: *High Plains History.*) p. 65.

[145] Pearl Morrison. Interview. 1936.

[146] Article. *Portales News-Tribune.* December 26, 1962.

Chapter 33
Homesteaders: Dobbs, Culberson, Birdwell

C.M. Dobbs, Well-driller

C. M. Dobbs, with his wife, daughter Jim, and son Buck came to Eastern New Mexico in 1898 to drill wells for the DZ Ranch, then owned by the Curtiss Brothers. They lived in a trailer house built on a wagon frame at the DZ hearquarters.

Jim, later Mrs. F. T. Burke, remembered, "His well-drilling rig was horse-powered. Three horses or mules were hitched to a beam which they moved around a circle. The boom was geared to the digging tool."[147]

While C. M. worked for the DZ, he also kept busy drilling wells for other large ranches. After the little town of Portales began to develop, C. M. partnered with Dr. Pearce to buy out Josh Morrison's store and start a mercantile store on the main street of town. Afterwards the partners, Pearce and Dobbs, built an adobe building on the lot adjoining the present News-Tribune and started a drug store. At one time there was also a butcher shop on the premises with a dirt cellar for keeping the meat cool.

The family moved to town where several homes in box tents had sprung up .Miss Jim related how she attended the first school which met in the railroad tool shed with Miss Sarah Malone as teacher. "The other pupils that I recall are Josie, Pearl, Hazel, and Joe Lang, Joe Deet, and my brother Buck."

The school didn't have textbooks, but used whatever books they could gather up from the community. The school in the tool shed had opened in the fall, but in January a new two-

---

[147] Jim Dobbs. interview. *Portales Daily News*. October 8, 1950.

room school was erected. J. A. Fairly and Miss Malone finished out the term and the next year, Miss Byrd Carter and Mr. Fairly taught classes.

Jim also remembered the first Sunday School which was held at the depot. A preacher from Roswell would come up on Saturday and visit everybody and then hold services. He carried a little folding organ with him for singing.

Jim worked for Dr. Pearce in the drug store and helped him care for his patients. She remembered that they sold patent medicines and Dr. Pearce filled his own prescriptions.[148]

Jim married F. T. Burke and they were the parents of seven children.

Mrs. Culberson

Mrs. S. F. Culberson was one of the unusual characters of the early days. So long was she connected with the schools of Portales that she gave high school diplomas to graduates whom she had taught when they were in the primary grades. Her long, conscientious service was of inestimable value to the public schools. All the children liked her, and learned better for that reason. As a true Southern aristocrat, she could have taken her place in any society. Yet she never complained at having to live in a small western town, nor at having to work hard for a living.

Born in Mississippi of a fine southern family, she was educated at Ward-Belmont school in Nashville. Soon after finishing school, she married a Mr. Morgan. After a few years of happy married life, he died, leaving her with two small children, a boy and a girl.

She was engaged to be married again to the lieutenant governor of Mississippi, when she went to Texas to visit friends. In Texas she met Dr. Culberson, a handsome Civil War veteran, six feet four inches tall. Once when he and his equally stalwart brother marched in a parade of ex-soldiers in Atlanta, a bystander exclaimed, "No wonder the south held out so long, if men like that made up the army!" We are not surprised to hear that the handsome soldier won the young widow's heart and that the

---

[148] Jim Dobbs Burke. interview by Rose White. 1940.

lieutenant governor, with all the honor and social prestige that went with marriage to him, were discarded.

In or about 1900 Dr. Culberson and his wife moved to Portales, then a new town consisting of two or three stores, a wagon yard, a depot and a dozen houses. During the latter days of his life, Dr. Culberson suffered from a broken hip and spent his days in a wheelchair.

Mrs. Culberson faced with the task of earning the living taught school in Portales. She proved a great success at this work, and was beloved by pupils and parents alike. An entertaining speaker, she could hold the high school pupils spellbound for as long as she chose to talk to them. Her four years as county school superintendent brought the county schools to a new level of efficiency.

It was a great loss to Portales when Mrs. Culberson moved to Tiaban. She spent her last years in Santa Fe in the home of her son. She ended her days in a wheelchair because of a broken hip, just as had her husband. How often she must have thought of her happy days in Portales and of her many loyal friends there.[149]

Sid Birdwell

Sid Birdwell came to the new little town of Portales with his family in 1899. He wrote in a letter to the Portales News-Tribune: "My father moved his family to Portales in 1899. I was eleven years old; you can figure the remainder. I was working for the Santa Fe as telegraph operator when the present station was built and put in service.

"When we arrived there, it had two stores and three saloons. I attended school in the PV and NE Ry. [Portales Valley and Northeastern Railway] hand car house. There were about a dozen of us brats. A teacher by name of Miss Malone was hired by our parents to teach us. She came from Wichita Falls, Texas.

---

[149] Rose White. "Early Day Pioneers." *Portales Daily News.* September 14, 1937.

166

"My father was the first elected County Clerk of Roosevelt County. I would like to visit the old town once more.[150]

"One time I was working for old man W.E. Stewart in his livery stable and feed store and an order had been placed for a single rig to be brought to Bill Carson's Saloon about nine at night, I harnessed the horse to a nice single rig and took it to his saloon and after hitching it to the rack, went in to tell him it was there. He was setting with his head on a card table. When I touched him, he tumbled; he was dead. Tom Longacer had killed him, it was later learned."[151]

---

[150] Georgiana Cooper. "Idle Chatter." *Portales News-Tribune.* August 9, 1965.

[151] Sid Birdwell. letter to Rose White. September 26. 1967.

Chapter 34
The First Christmas

In 1899 the new little town of Portales was only one year old when the few settlers decided to have a Christmas celebration. Picnics and hayrides were common, but there had never been a get-together that included all the townspeople and farmers and ranchers from all over the county.

This is the way that the town looked in December of 1899. There were the beginnings of two or three general stores, a few saloons, wagon yards, a hotel, lumber yard, blacksmith shop, barber shop, and many businesses still operating out of wagons. Several homes were completed, and more were under construction. There were numerous tent houses and many adobe or sod dwellings on the surrounding farms znd ranches.

A school and a Sunday school had been organized, but there was no doctor, no druggist, no law or courts, no land office, no churches, no undertaker, no lights or running water. The mail still came in by train and was left in a box at Uncle Josh's store for everyone to look over and pick out his own.

The celebration was planned for months ahead of time, and the word went out to all the far flung farms and ranches. Inquiries came in to Uncle Josh about various presents; toys, dishes, tools, and so forth. If he couldn't supply them, they were ordered from Amarillo or Colorado City, Texas.

Some of the men took a team of horses and a wagon and went to the brakes up near Tucumcari to get a tree. It took them three days to go and find a suitable tree and bring it back. They set it up in the railroad depot, as it was the only building in town with a room big enough to hold everybody. The depot was a frame building with a corrugated roof that stood across the end of what is now Main Street.

That afternoon Miss Ella Turner, Mrs. Woodcock, and other ladies popped popcorn and strung it. Some of them filled sacks with candy and nuts, and added an apple and orange in each. They decorated the tree with the garlands of popcorn, bright red apples, candy canes, and little toys. Tiny candles were placed in little tin holders and secured to the branches of the tree.

There were piles of presents stacked under the tree; some were jokes and some were nice gifts. There were saddles, bridles, potatoes, spurs, onions, silverware, and dishes; gifts for everyone. According to Miss Ella, there must have been $500 worth of presents, so they locked the door carefully when they went home to supper.

People began arriving right after supper; old ones and young ones and middle-aged. The ranchers and cowboys left their teams at the wagon yards and came on to the depot. Some of them had come as much as fifty miles to be at the celebration.

Ora Wood recalled the night with shining eyes: "Soon the waiting room was crowded with noisy, jolly people. The room was almost as bright as a sunny day for the depot agent had managed to get an engine headlight to light up the party, and it was fastened up on the wall opposite the tree.

"Everybody was talking and laughing and milling around. Suddenly, a loud clanking was heard on the tin roof. 'That is Santa's sleigh with his reindeer,' said someone; though we learned afterwards that some of the big boys were just dragging an iron chain across the tin roof.

"Sure enough, in a minute we heard a banging at the door, and when it was opened, Santa Claus came riding right into the room mounted on a little gray donkey. 'I guess the reindeer couldn't have stood the heat of this wood stove,' I heard one of the mothers say to her little boy.

"Santa didn't have on his red suit, but he had bushy, white whiskers. And he wore a long overcoat trimmed with white cotton for fur. You could see that he had cowboy boots on his feet, and his hat looked just like the one Frank Boykin wore when he was herding cattle. Come to think of it, his voice was like Frank's too; but that didn't bother anybody; and they all laughed and began pushing the little children forward to speak to him.

"He had a big tow-sack full of presents, and right away he started handing them out. Then all the young boys helped him by running back and forth delivering presents from the piles at the foot of the tree."[152]

What were some of the presents they received that night?

Mrs. Wood got a sidesaddle and a Navajo saddle blanket and a pretty set of six red tumblers with a pitcher to match.

Little Eddie White, her son, got a comb and brush in a leather case; and Bill, who was only four years old, got a little metal fire wagon with two prancing horses to pull it.

Mrs. Morrison got a fancy castor set to put on the table with bottles for oil, vinegar, salt, pepper, and sugar. Many years later, she willed it to Ora Wood, and that was the start of Grandma Wood's fantastic collection of Western memorabilia.

Buck Dobbs gave his sister, Jim Dobbs Burke, a little silver heart with a red stone on a silver chain. Lizzie Boykin got a pretty gold jewelry box from Sid.

Mattie Mitchell Carr, received a pair of glass vases to set on shelves on either side of a mirror. And Miss Ella Turner got a beautiful bouquet of white chrysanthemums from Mrs. Josh Morrison. Sam Birdwell, the railroad agent, gave Mrs. Wood a green glass vase.

All the little girls got sets of cups and saucers from John and Henry Hughes, who had a small store. One of the men got a ladies' bustle. Everyone: man, woman, and child got a sack of candy.

After the festivities were over, some families drove home in their wagons and buggies, some spent the night with friends or at the hotel, and some camped out in the nearby wagon yard with their teams.

According to several of the old-timers, this was one of the brightest spots in their sometimes hard and dreary lives: a Christmas so full of hope and joy and goodwill, that it would probably not be surpassed for the rest of their days.

This Christmas seems to illustrate the character and good will of the first settlers. They did not have much, but they were

---

[152] Ora Wood. interview with Rose White. 1930.

ready and willing to share what they did have. The hard-bitten old ranchers were beginning to accept the nesters and become friends with them.

One likes to think that this spirit lives on in Portales. Over the years, many newcomers and new ideas have been accepted. The university has brought in many students of diverse cultures, and they have been integrated into our town. The city has grown from Uncle Josh's one little store to a prosperous community and it continues to grow.[153]

Gifts from the first Christmas Tree on the plains. 1899.
Burns Collection.

---

[153] Rose White. "The FIrst Christmas in Portales." *Portales Daily News.* December 22, 1949.

Chapter 35
Civilization Comes to the Llano

In 1869 Lincoln County was carved out of the Territory of New Mexico. It encompassed 17,000,000 acres and included all the southeastern quarter of New Mexico. In it were the counties that would later become Roosevelt, Chaves, Lea, Eddy, and parts of Curry, DeBaca, Otero, Torrance, and Socorro. In 1889 Chavez County was formed including much of the eastern plains. It was not until 1903 that Roosevelt County was formed and 1909 when Curry became a county. New Mexico did not become a state until 1912.

The Pecos Valley and Northeastern Railroad, or Peavine, as it was locally called, had reached the area in 1898, and as the nesters arrived and organized schools and churches near their claims, little communities began to spring up all over the plains. The Santa Fe Railroad began to build the Belen Cut-Off west from Texico in 1906 and soon afterwards the roundhouse and the city of Clovis were laid out at what had been Riley's Switch. The towns of Texico, New Mexico and Farwell, across the state line in Texas, were settled to the east on the railroad; Elida and Kenna on the northwest; and Melrose and others west on the new tracks. Towns springing up south of Portales were Dora, Tatum and several other smaller towns.[154]

When Roosevelt County was made from the north part of Chaves County in 1903, immediately there arose the need for County officials: Commissioners, County Clerk, Sheriff, and so forth. Surprisingly enough, there were plenty of local people who

---

[154] Kilmer, Harold and Don McAlavy. *Curry County High Plains Historical Foundation.* (Dallas: Taylor Publishing Co. 1978.) p. 57.

were capable of filling the new offices. While one is tempted to imagine that all the nesters were ignorant newcomers, a great number of them were educated men and women. Many of them had come West in search of better health. The "lungers," those suffering from tuberculosis, usually got well and lived to a good old age, using their knowledge of teaching or bookkeeping or surveying to help improve the new community.

As the homesteaders began to feel that they could make permanent homes on the Llano Estacado, they organized churches and schools for their children. In Portales the first school was in a railroad tool shed and served the few children, including Eddie and Bill White, who were the right age to attend. But it was only two years until a two-room school house was built just east of where L.L. Brown School now is located. Mr. John Fairly, a cousin of the Turner family, became the first superintendent. Miss Sarah Malone, who had taught in the tool shed, taught the lower grades.[155]

Before there were any church buildings, the people held a "Union Sunday School" in the warehouse room of Blankenship & Woodcock's General Store on Main Street. Miss Ella Turner, the first Secretary, has said, "The benches were made of boards laid on little kegs. I've often wondered what was in the kegs." To which Mrs. Bob Wood replied, "Why, don't you know? There was whiskey in those kegs!"[156]

The Presbyterian Church soon organized its members and built a church, and the Baptist and Methodist Churches promptly followed suit.

Before Jim Stone's bank opened, business men and ranchers kept their surplus money in the big safe at the Blankenship & Woodcock General Store. People were so honest in those days that a receipt was seldom needed: contracts were agreed to without any written paper. "A man's word was as good as his bond," was certainly true of the majority of the business men of the Staked Plains.

---

[155] Rose White.   Speech. "The New Little Town of Portales."

[156] Ora Wood. interview by Rose White. 1932.

In the outlying districts the schools had a hard time. Often there was only money enough for three months of school. A teacher would hold school in one area, then in another for three more months, then, perhaps in a third one, thus earning a full year's salary. And the pupils would earn a full year's credit, for they would follow the teacher from school to school. Since they often rode horseback for as much as twenty miles, it seemed only a little longer ride to go on to another session.

In the space of seven short years, the little town of Portales had grown into a fine business center, with three general stores, three hotels, a barber shop, a restaurant, a post office, a drug store, seven saloons, and several stores operating out of box tents. With such flimsy buildings, there were many fires, by accident or design, especially after Proibition made selling liquor illegal.

The Roosevelt County Courthouse was completed in 1904, and the records of patents, deeds, and other papers were transferred from Roswell. With a railroad and a telegraph to keep people in touch with the outside world, the worst of the pioneering days were over. In 1909 the City of Portales was incorporated. Ranchers no longer had to make the long trail drive to Kansas. Farms were producing feed and grain for the cattle. Supplies were brought in by train, not by twice-yearly wagons and local businesses stocked every kind of merchandise. Farmers were learning about irrigation. Churches and schools dotted the county. People had found that with perseverence and hard work, a wonderful life could be had on the High Plains.

In spite of the hardships, most early settlers looked back on their former struggles with fondness. Billy Dixon lived through all the trials and hardships of the early days, including the Buffalo Wallow fight and the Adobe Walls encounter, in which he was renowned for the long shot with his 50 Sharp's long rifle that helped end the seige.

Of his many difficult encounters, he expressed what would have been the feelings of many of the pioneers. "I am often questioned about my experiences on the frontier, as if the life had been filled with unbearable hardships, to be shunned and forgotten. Gladly would I live it all over again, such is my cast of mind and my hunger for the freedom of the big wide places. I would run the risks and endure all the hardships that were naturally ours just for the contentment and freedom to be found in such an outdoor life. I should be unspeakably happy once more to feast on buffalo meat and other wild game cooked on a campfire, to eat sour dough biscuit and drink black coffee from a quart tin cup."[157]

This brings us to a consideration of the character of the cowboys, ranchers, nesters, and even the outlaws of the Western Plains Country. In all the stories of stagecoach robberies, train holdups or cattle rustlers, there is no tale of any robbery of a lonely homestead, nor any rape of a farm woman who was by herself while her husband was away at work.

It makes us think of Buster DeGraftenreid's summation of the character of the pioneers on the Llano Estacado: "We had to go clear to Lincoln or Las Vegas to court; but it didn't matter, as we didn't settle our differences in court, anyway; because a man was a real man in them days or he didn't last long, and all the women was ladies."[158]

---

[157] Olive K. Dixon. *The Life of 'Billy' Dixon.* (Austin: State House Press. 1987.) p. 239.

[158] Buster DeGraftenreid. interview by Rose White. 1940.

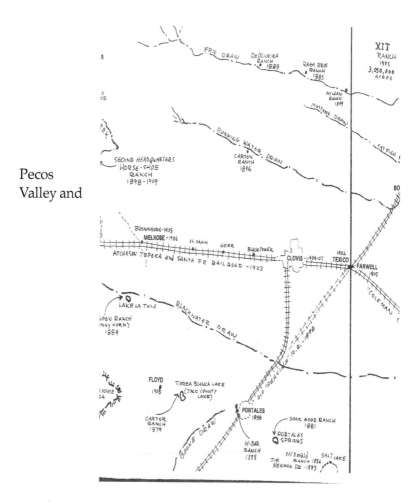

Pecos
Valley and

Northeastern Railroad and the Atchison Topeka and Santa Fe
Railroad in 1906. Courtesy of Harold Kilmer and Don McAlavy.
High Plains History. 1980.

Portales street about 1903. Courtesy of Portales
News-Tribune.

Portales about 1906. Courtesy ENMU Golden Library Special
Collections

First Grand Jury in Roosevelt County 1904. Burns Collection.

Ora Wood on her sidesaddle ready for the Old-Timers Day
Parade. 1935.

Afterward

When the old Whippet car drove up to the dilapidated farm house, twenty-eight year old Rosalie Powers White had no idea what kind of life she was entering. She had been raised in the enterprising town of Las Vegas, New Mexico, just a few blocks from the plaza. Her parents had come to Nogal from Kentucky in the early 1900s to supervise a gold mine. They later moved to Las Vegas when the mine played out.

Her father, Stephen Powers, surveyed many of the highways in Northern New Mexico and engineered the building of the flume which brought water from the canyon to Las Vegas. He then worked for the Agua Pura Company supervising their ponds on the Gallinas River and the ice-cutting in the winter. At one time the Powers family managed the historic Plaza Hotel and the family lived on the premises. Las Vegas was modern and sophisticated, being one of the oldest towns in Northern New Mexico.

Rose received her teaching certificate from Highlands Normal School in 1918, and began her career at the age of seventeen. She taught English, Spanish, and Higher Mathematics at Vaughn and Santa Rosa, and it was in Santa Rosa that she met R. E. "Eddie" White.

Eddie was employed by the New Mexico Tax Commission to travel the state assessing property. He had lost an arm in France in World War I, so he could not return to his profession as railroad engineer. He secured the job with the tax commission and traveled the state, while continuing to care for his aging parents in Portales.

When Eddie and Rose were married in Tucumcari in 1923 and drove to Portales where they were to live with Eddie's parents, Rose's apprehension turned to reality when they arrived at the farm four miles north of town. The Woods were living in primitive conditions just as they had on the H-Bar Ranch in the 1890s. Their diet was mostly beans and beef with a little canned fruit and tomatoes. Mrs. Wood made her dresses out of flowered feed sacks; a wagon was their only form of transportation; and they were still using cow chips for fuel.

Ora and Bob Wood were pioneers in the true sense of the word. Bob was a typical old-time cowboy. He had left home at a very young age and as a consequence was largely uneducated, but was highly efficient in the business of raising and herding cattle.

Although the Wood family lived like "pore folks," they had managed to buy up a sizable portion of land on the west side of town. This land was subdivided and became the Wood Edition.

The Woods were kind and friendly to the new bride, and Rose soon adjusted to the different standard of living. Eddie gave up his job and the newlyweds moved out to a shack in the sandhills to homestead. They rode out to their claim on horseback for a few days every month, and spent the rest of the time on the Woods' farm.

Two years later after proving up on the claim, Eddie and his brother Bill built the Lilac Park Grocery and Service Station, and Rose and Eddie lived in an apartment in the back of the store. Behind the store was a "camp ground," a row of apartments similar to a motel. After moving to town, Rose taught for one year at Portales High School before their first child, R. E. Jr., "Bobby," was born in their home in the back of Lilac Park.

Two years later, Eddie bought a triangular block of land containing a house into which he moved his ailing parents. Next to it he built a two-bedroom house where Mary Ruth "Ruthie" and James Gordon "Jimmy" were born.

From the first Rose had been aware that she was living in the midst of a pioneer family; and as she became more acquainted with the townspeople, she saw that there was no written history of the immediate area. This was an area that had been largely ignored. Much was written about the more densely populated area to the west along the Rio Grande and the Pecos Rivers. Towns such as Santa Fe, Las Vegas, and Ft. Sumner had long been centers of trade and military operations, and as such, merited considerable interest. But the Llano Estacado in Eastern New Mexico and West Texas was the last frontier.

She realized that if someone did not write down the first-hand knowledge possessed by these remaining pioneers, it would soon be lost. She began to write down the stories of Mr. and Mrs. Wood and to interview their early-day friends. She also collected books of southwestern history and began to correspond with historians.

We had many visitors in our home as I was growing up, some cowboys, some authors, some acquaintances from Rose's girlhood in Las Vegas. There were cowboys: Jack Potter, Mac McNulty, Joe Beasley, Dan McFatter, Cooley Urton, Joe Boren, and Buster DeGraftenreid. Some of the homesteaders were Ella Turner, Jim Dobbs, Grace Scott Henderson, Mattie Mitchell Carr, Helen Lindsey, and Sid Birdwell. I remember old friends Fabiola Cabeza de Baca Gilbert who wrote *The Good Life* and *We Fed Them Cactus*; Eve Ball, author of *Bob Crosby, Ma'am Jones of the Pecos*, and several books about the Mescalero Apaches; Grace Barker Wilson, sister of Elliot and S. Omar, authors of poetry and New Mexico wildlife; Erna Fergusson, author of *Our Southwest* and *Murder and Mystery in New Mexico*; and Dr. Matt Pearce, who received assistance from Rose on his book, *New Mexico Place Names*.

As her knowledge grew, Rose began to write newspaper articles about the early days, and became a frequent speaker at organizational meetings and in school classrooms. She contributed to the "Western Folklore Publication," the "New Mexico Folklore Record," and served as president of the New Mexico Folklore Society in 1948-49.

She began to organize her interviews and research into a book, but she died in 1969 with her task unfinished. Rose was honored in 2008 by having a New Mexico Highway Marker erected in her honor.

After Eddie died in 1975, I became heir to all Rose's books and papers, and they rested in their filing cabinets and bookshelves until I retired from teaching in 1991. In order to preserve her work, and have it available for others, I have put together her articles and interviews just as she wrote them, with minor editing and research.

Of course, there were many other ranchers and homesteaders that have not been named in this book whose stories are just as worthy of remebrance. I have included only those whose words are directly taken from personal interviews and letters and from recognized historians. I hope that the accounts that are related here will give a fair picture of what life was like for the early settlers on the High Plains. My main goal is to illustrate the character of these first settlers and their hardships by telling their stories in their own words.

By putting this book together, I feel I am fulfilling a commitment to my mother and also her commitment to the people and history of Eastern New Mexico, the adopted home she came to love so dearly.

Rose Powers White. About 1949.

Acknowledgements

Many people have helped me in bringing this book to publication. First among them are my children, Mike Jr., Jo, Pat, Jackie, Ike, Karen, and Becky, who have supported me with proof-reading and encouragement. Mike has been especially helpful, spending many hours in research and computer expertise.

Gene Bundy of the Special Collections of the Golden Library at Eastern New Mexico University has aided me with editing, location of photographs, and advice on publication..

Descendants of local pioneers, David Stone, Jayne Taylor, Tish McDaniel, Pat Boone and Jim Warnica have allowed me to quote their parents and grandparents and Lawanda Calton has permitted me to use her painting on the cover of this book.

Ruth White Burns

Author Biography

Mary Ruth (always called Ruth or Ruthie) White Burns was born March 11, 1929 in Portales, New Mexico to Robert Edward "Eddie" White and Rosalie Pierce Powers White. She grew up with her two brothers, R. E. Jr. "Bobbie" and James Gordon "Jimmy" White at the family home, next door to her grand-parents, Robert Lee "Bob" Wood and Ora Powell White Wood.

She attended Eastern New Mexico College until 1950 when she married Michael Dan Burns and left school to become a homemaker. Their first child, Mike Jr., was born in 1951, followed by Patrick Neil, Dwight Edward "Ike", and Rebecca Rose. The couple started their own business, Burns Wholesale, selling candy, tobacco and restaurant supplies throughout the surrounding area.

Ruth worked in the wholesale business and concentrated on raising the four children until she returned to ENMU to complete her degree in Education. She also studied a semester in Saltillo, Mexico, and received her endorsement in Bilingual Education. She taught second grade at La Casita School in the first Bilingual program in Clovis. For several years, she served on the New Mexico State Bilingual Advisory Commission.

Over the years, Ruth worked on transcribing her mother's articles, interviews, and letters and combining them into a book. She has published articles in local newspapers and the New Mexico Magazine. At present she lives in Clovis, New Mexico.

Ruth Burns with Rose Powers White Historical Marker. 2010.

Bibliography

Armstrong, Helen Lindsey. Interview by Mike Burns Jr. 1973.

Barker, S. Omar. *Jack Potter's Courtin' and Jack Potter's Talkin' Steer.* Phoenix: Miner Cowboy Productions. 1998.

Beasley, Joe. Interview by Rose White. 1936.

Birdwell, Sid. Letter to Rose White. September 26,1967.

Blythe, Dee.. "Melrose Pioneer Once traded Horses with Geronimo." *Clovis Eveing News. May 31, 1937.*

Boone III, Patrick H. *An Oral History.* Dictated 1986.

Boone IV, Patrick H. Interview by Ruth Burns. 2011.

Boykin, Lizzie. Interview by Rose White, 1949.

Burke, Jim Dobbs. Interview by Rose White,1939.
_____ Interview. *Portales Daily News. October 8, 1950.*

Burns, Mike Jr. Interview of Helen Lindsey Armstrong.
_____*Ghost Steer* poem.

Burns, Pat. Drawing. *Billly the Kid at Portales Springs.* 2000. Drawing. *Ghost Steer.*

Calton, Lawanda. Painting. *Los Portales.* 2012.

Carlson, Paul H. *The Buffalo Soldier Tragedy of 1877.* College Station. Texas A&M Press. 2003.

Carr, Mattie Lang Mitchell. Interview by Rose White. 1936.

Cass County Historical Center. Cass County, Missouri.

Clovis News Journal. Articles.

Collison, Frank. Amarillo: *Amarillo Globe News*, Mar. 2, 1941.

Cook, John R. *The Border and The Buffalo*. Topeka: Crane & Co, 1907.

Cook, Jim with Dr. T. M. Pearce. *Lane of the Llano*. Boston: Little, Brown, & Co. 1936.

Cooper, Georgiana. "Idle Chatter." *Portales News-Tribune.* August 9,1965.

Daily New Mexican. March 3, 1871.

Degraftenreid, Buster. Letters to Rose White. 1940.

Dixon, Olive K. *The LIfe of Billy Dixon*. Austin: State House Press. 1987.

Dobie, J. Frank. *"Belling the Lead Steer."* Jack Potter, *Lead Steer and Other Tales*. Clayton: Leader Press. 1939.
_____ *The Longhorns*. Boston: Little, Brown & Co, 1941.

Dunlap, W. O. Jr. Interview by Rose White. 1940.
_____Article. *Portales News-Tribune.*

Eastern New Mexico Uiversity Golden Library Special Collections. Photographs.

Easton, Robert and Mackenzie Brown. *Lord of the Beasts*. Tuscon: University of Arizona Press. 1961.

Grayson County, Texas, GenWeb. "Buster DeGraftenreid." June 6, 1938.

Garrett, Pat. *The Authentic Life of BIlly The Kid*. New York: McMillan Co. 1927.

Greaves, Annie King. *Six Miles to the Windmill*. Portales: 1976.

Greaves, Gordon King. "By the Way." *Portales News-Tribune. May 15, 1962.*

Greaves, J. G. "Spud Spouts." *Portales News-Tribune.* No Date

Gunn, Marjorie. Speech to Roosevelt County Historical Society. 1990.

Haley, J. Evetts. *Charles Goodnight*. Norman: University of Olkahoma Press, 1936.
_____*George W. Littlefield, Texan.* Norman: University of Oklahoma Press, 1943.
_____"Jim Cook on the Frontiers of Fantasy." Amarillo. *The Shamrock.* Spring. 1964.
_____*The XIT Ranch of Texas.* Norman: University of Oklahoma Press, 1929.

Hawkins, Susan. "James 'Buster' DeGraftenreid." *Grayson Co. TXGenWeb*, June 6, 1938.

Henderson, Grace Scott. interview with Rose White. 1936

Jones, Arthur. Interview with Rose White. 1945.

Kilmer, Harold & Don McAlavy. *High Plains History.* U.S.A.: High Plains Historical Press, 1980.
_____ *Curry County, High Plains Historical Foundation.* Dallas: Taylor Publishing Co. 1978.

Lone Jack Historical Society. Lone Jack, Missouri.

McAlavy, Don.*High Plains History.* U.S.A.: High Plains Historical Press, 1980.
_____ *Curry County, High Plains Historical Foundation.* Dallas: Taylor Publishing Co. 1978.

McFatter, Dan. Interview by Rose White, 1939.
_____Letters to Rose White. 1936 to 1940.

McGowen, Ruth. Interview by Rose White, 1936.

Mooar, J. Wright. *Buffalo Days.* Abilene: Statehouse Press. McMurray University. 2005.

Morrison, Pearl. Interview by Rose White. 1949.

Neeley, Bill. *Quanah Parker and His People.* Slaton. Brazos Press. 1986.

Nita Stewart Haley Memorial Library. *Cook Family Group Record.* Midland.

Pearce, Dr. J. S. Obituary. *Portales Daily-News.March, 1941.*
_____ Dr. J. S. Statement to Bryan J. Moore. September 3, 1922.

Portales News-Tribune. "Jim Miller, 'Meanest Man in West' Figured in Swindle Here." September 21, 1952.
_____ "Jack County Terrell Started Riding Ranges Here in 1894." *Portales News Tribune.* 1952

Potter, Jack. *Lead Steer and Other Tales.* Clayton: Leader Press, 1939.
_____ *Cattle Trails of the Old West.* Clayton: Laura R. Krehbiel. 1935.
_____"Tragedies of the Portales Road." Clayton: *Union County Leader.,* 1942.
_____ Interview by Rose White. 1948.
_____Letters to Rose White 1940 to 1950.

Redfield Georgia B. "*W.G. Urton.*" WPA Federal Writers Project, January 20, 1939.

Riley, Della. Article. *Portales News-Tribune.* May 14, 1950.

Siringo, Charles. *A Texas Cowboy*. Chicago: M. Umbdenstock & Co., 1885.

Stone, David. Interview by Ruth Burns, 2009.

Taylor, Jayne Wilcox, *Kenna, a Ranching Community*. Elida: 1991.

Turner, Ella. Interview by Rose White, 1936.

Urton, W. C. "Cooley." Letters to Rose White. 1940-1950.
_____ "Roundup on the Pecos." *New Mexico Stockman,* June 1949.

Warnica, Jim. Letter to Ruth Burns. 2011.

White, Rose. "Banks in the Early Days." *Portales News.*
_____ "Cowboy Humor."*New Mexico Folklore Society.*
_____ "The Ghost Steer." Speech. *New Mexico Folklore Society.*
    1948.
_____ "A Man Was a Real Man." Speech. N.M. Folklore Society.
_____ "New Mexico Place Names." *New Mexico Folklore*
    Sociaty. 1948.
_____ "Portales in 1880." Speech. Rotary Club.
_____ "Stone Age to Space Age." Speech. Portales Women's Club.
_____ "The First Christmas Tree." *Portales News.*
_____ "The Sourdough Biscuit." *Western Folklore.* April, 1956.
_____ "Too Pore To Leave." *Portales News. 1950.*

White, R. E. "Eddie." Interviews by Rose White.1932 to 1939.

Whitlock, V. H. *Cowboy Life on the Llano Estacado.* Norman: University of Oklahoma Press, 1970.

Winfrey, Dr. Hadley. Letter to Lincoln Coounty Commissioners. July 1887.

Wood, Ora. Interviews by Rose White. 1932 to 1939.

Wood, R. L. "Bob." Interviews by Rose White. 1932 to 1939.

Appendix

Humorous postcards from the 1920s erroneously labeling the H-Bar Ranch as the place where Billy the Kid was taken after his death, dressing up local residents as Indians and drug-store cowboys, and depicting an irrigation ditch as a means of transportation.

X-Bar Ranch to Which "Billy the Kid" Was Taken After Being Shot, Portales, N. M.

H— Ranch Where the Outlaw "Billy the Kid" was taken After Being Shot, Portales, New Mexico.

Court House and Original Settlers, Portales, N. M.

Rapid Transportation on the Desert, Portales, N. M.

Made in the USA
Lexington, KY
04 October 2012